DOREEN VIRTUE

Praise God in the Storm

Comforting Encouragement 30-Day Devotional for Christian Women

First published by Amazing Grace 2025

Copyright © 2025 by Doreen Virtue

All rights reserved. No part of this publication may be reproduced, stored or transmitted in any form or by any means, electronic, mechanical, photocopying, recording, scanning, or otherwise without written permission from the publisher. It is illegal to copy this book, post it to a website, or distribute it by any other means without permission.

Christian Standard Bible (CSB) Publisher: Holman Bible Publishers Copyright: © 2017 by Holman Bible Publishers Fair Use Statement: The verses in this work are used under the Fair Use copyright law.

English Standard Version (ESV) Publisher: Crossway Copyright: © 2001 by Crossway Fair Use Statement: The verses in this work are used under the Fair Use copyright law.

King James Version (KJV) Publisher: Various publishers (original 1611 edition is public domain, but modern editions are published by different houses like Thomas Nelson or Cambridge University Press) Copyright: Public domain for the original 1611 edition, but modern editions may have specific copyright for certain elements (e.g., introduction, commentary) Fair Use Statement: The verses in this work are used under the Fair Use copyright law.

Legacy Standard Bible (LSB) Publisher: The Lockman Foundation Copyright © by The Lockman Foundation Fair Use Statement: The verses in this work are used under the Fair Use copyright law.

New American Standard Bible (NASB) Publisher: The Lockman Foundation Copyright: © 1995 by The Lockman Foundation Fair Use Statement: The verses in this work are used under the Fair Use copyright law.

New International Version (NIV) Publisher: Zondervan (a division of HarperCollins) Copyright: © 2011 by Biblica, Inc.™ Fair Use Statement: The verses in this work are used under the Fair Use copyright law.

New King James Version (NKJV) Publisher: Thomas Nelson Copyright: © 1987 by Thomas Nelson Fair Use Statement: The verses in this work are used under the Fair Use copyright law.

The New Living Translation (NLT) Publisher: Tyndale House Publishers, Inc. Copyright © by Tyndale House Publishers, Inc. Fair Use Statement: The verses in this work are used under the Fair Use copyright law.

World English Bible (WEB) Publisher: Public Domain (Originally published by the World English Bible project) Copyright: Public Domain Fair Use Statement: The verses in this work are used under the Fair Use copyright law.

First edition

This book was professionally typeset on Reedsy.
Find out more at reedsy.com

Contents

Introduction: Praising God in the Storm	1
Chapter 1: God is our Refuge	4
Chapter 2: When Your Faith is Tested	8
Chapter 3: The Honor of Suffering	11
Chapter 4: Complaining and Praying	16
Chapter 5: Momentary Light Affliction	20
Chapter 6: God's Refining Process	23
Chapter 7: Jesus our Lighthouse and Anchor	26
Chapter 8: His Grace is Sufficient	29
Chapter 9: Hope in the Midst of Suffering	32
Chapter 10: Uplifted with Hope	36
Chapter 11: Count it All Joy	39
Chapter 12: Cast Your Cares on Him	42
Chapter 13: Thy Will be Done	45
Chapter 14: Blessings Out of Adversity	50
Chapter 15: More Than Conquerors	53
Chaper 16: God of all Comfort	56
Chapter 17: Jesus, the Suffering Servant	59
Chapter 18: We Do Not Lose Heart	62
Chapter 19: God is the Strength of Your Heart	65
Chapter 20: Rejoicing Together	70
Chapter 21: Joyful in Hope	73
Chapter 22: Rest in Christ	76
Chapter 23: Don't Worry, Pray Instead	79
Chapter 24: Hope in Eternal Glory	82

Chapter 25: The Indwelling Holy Spirit	84
Chapter 26: Wings like Eagles	87
Chapter 27: Delegating and Sharing Your Burdens	91
Chapter 28: Patiently Waiting on God's Timing	94
Chapter 29: Take Up Your Cross	97
Chapter 30: Comfort in Christ	100
Afterword: Hold On to His Promises	104
About the Author	105
Also by Doreen Virtue	106

Introduction: Praising God in the Storm

"He will wipe away every tear from their eyes, and death shall be no more, neither shall there be mourning, nor crying, nor pain anymore, for the former things have passed away." Revelation 21:4

Have ever felt like your life is one long storm? Perhaps you're in a challenging situation right now that seems impossible, even though you realize that with Christ all things are possible.

I've been there, dear sister! And in some ways, my life became more stormy since God saved me in 2017. Since that time, both my parents passed away and I've lost family, friends, pets, and had financial struggles. Yet, through it all - and hopefully you can relate to this - there's a bright warm light of Christ's love in my heart. He may not always stop the storms in our lives, but He's always there to encourage and strengthen us.

The Bible teaches that God uses our storms to help us to grow, learn, and draw closer to Him. You may wonder if there's an easier way for God to accomplish this, yet we also need to acknowledge that God is our sovereign Creator. Just as you love your children and only want what's best for them, so too does your Heavenly Father.

We all have moments when life doesn't make sense, when the waves of struggle feel like they're crashing over us, and we desperately want them to stop. We think of Job losing everyone and everything in a single day, and then questioning, *"Why, God?"*

And yet, in the middle of horrendous suffering, Job said:

> *"Naked I came from my mother's womb, and naked I will depart. The Lord gave and the Lord has taken away; may the name of the Lord be praised."* (Job 1:20-21).

Job had just lost his children, his health, and his livestock - and he praised the Lord's name in the middle of this turmoil!

Well, there's so much to praise God for, isn't there? No matter what we're going through, we can rejoice that our triune co-equal co-eternal Father, Son, and Holy Spirit provide protection, provision, wisdom, strength, and most of all salvation. Jesus, fully God and fully man, came to earth and lived a sinless life.

We humans have a fallen nature that can lead us to sin against our Holy God. But God, in His mercy and grace, saved us because Jesus took the wrath that we all deserve for our sins. After Jesus died upon the cross, He was buried for 3 days and then He bodily rose from the dead. Jesus conquered sin and death for those who believe in the Gospel! Believers have their sins forgiven by Jesus' perfect righteousness. Praise God!

I remember when I was a new Christian and enduring deep sorrow and fear. It was suffocating like I couldn't breathe! God in His providence, led me to Isaiah 61:3 in the King James Bible. When I read about the "spirit of heaviness" in this verse, it felt like answered prayer because that's exactly how I was feeling! Of course, this was spiritual warfare which all Christians endure (Ephesians 6:10-18). This verse suggested that the garment of praise could be exchanged for the spirit of heaviness. Now this wasn't some superficial bargaining tool. I sincerely needed help in lifting the heaviness.

INTRODUCTION: PRAISING GOD IN THE STORM

So, I thought of everything for which I was grateful and I started praising God deeply and genuinely from my heart. Right away, I felt the heaviness lifting! We don't praise God to try to get something from Him. Praise is not some gimmicky tool. We should always be focused upon sincerely praising and glorifying God. Yet, that day of praising God was life-changing. The heaviness hasn't returned, thank you Lord!

In this 30-day devotional, we'll dive deeply into what the Bible says about praising God in the midst of the storm. We all know the Proverbs 3:5 exhortation to "Trust in the Lord with all of your heart," and in this devotional we'll explore practical applications to comfort and encourage you during seasons of struggles. We'll look at Biblical teachings about blessings that can come from trials, and how we can trust and praise God during these storms. I pray that this will be a comforting encouragement that will lift you up, no matter what you're enduring.

All glory to God, Doreen

Chapter 1: God is our Refuge

"God is our refuge and strength, a very present help in trouble. Therefore we will not fear though the earth gives way, though the mountains be moved into the heart of the sea, though its waters roar and foam, though the mountains tremble at its swelling." (Psalm 46:1-3)

Sister, if you're going through a hardship right now, I empathize and know how you feel! It's emotionally, physically, and financially painful to go through a season of struggles. You may wonder, *"Why are you allowing this to happen to me, God?"* You might even speculate that you're being punished or abandoned. Yet, be assured that God is deeply involved in helping you through your challenges.

God knows that you're hurt, angry, and frightened during crises, as Psalm 34:18 reminds us:

"The Lord is near to the brokenhearted and saves those who are crushed in spirit."

So, you're not enduring this heartbreaking situation alone, dear sister. God is your refuge. A refuge is a place of safety or a sanctuary. God

CHAPTER 1: GOD IS OUR REFUGE

is your refuge and He offers comfort, strength and wisdom during trials, hardships, and emergencies. He is our safe haven Who shelters us during storms. This doesn't mean that the situation will instantly be resolved, but it does mean that God will be with you through painful ordeals.

After all, Jesus promised us that in this world we'll face hardship and trouble. He said:

> *"I have said these things to you, that in me you may have peace. In the world you will have tribulation. But take heart; I have overcome the world."*
> *(John 16:33).*

As Christians, Jesus said that we Christians are *in* this world, but we're not *of* the world as recorded in His High Priestly Prayer in John 17:14-16:

> *"I have given them your word, and the world has hated them because they are not of the world, just as I am not of the world. I do not ask that you take them out of the world, but that you keep them from the evil one. They are not of the world, just as I am not of the world."*

As Christ-followers, we've been set apart from the world. We are part of God's Kingdom while we're living on earth and we will continue to be in His Kingdom for eternity.

Jesus said that the world hates us Christians because we aren't of this world. We are in Christ, Whom the world has rejected. Jesus also clarified that He's not praying for us to be removed from the world, but to be protected from the evil one while we're here.

Sometimes it's tempting to think, *"Well then why don't you just take me home now, Lord, so I don't have to endure the suffering on earth any longer?"* Yet, while we're here, we have work to do on behalf of God's Kingdom. Every Christian is given the Great Commission to fulfill by sharing the Gospel, making disciples, baptizing them in the name of the Father and of the Son and of the Holy Spirit, and teaching them to observe all that Jesus commanded us (c.f., Matthew 28:18-20).

Jesus also comforts us with His promise: "I am with you always, to the end of the age." (Matthew 28:20). He assures us that His presence is with those who believe the Gospel. As you face the challenges of living in this hostile world, Jesus won't leave you. People may ignore you, abandon you, betray you, or be unsympathetic to your plight, but Jesus is right there with you through it all.

Jesus' presence is also a relationship promise. It means that He will never abandon you in your trials. Jesus said that the world that rejects the Gospel hates us Christians because we aren't of this world. Jesus clarified in this passage that He's not praying for us to be removed from the world, but to be protected from the evil one while we're here.

Jesus is with believers for eternity. It's comforting to think about the New Heaven, where there will be no more tears, sin, or sorrow! Jesus is our hope as we endure suffering for a little while here on earth. We must keep our eyes upon Him and our focus must be on eternity, as 1 Peter 5:10 emphasizes:

> *"And after you have suffered a little while, the God of all grace, who has called you to his eternal glory in Christ, will himself restore, confirm, strengthen, and establish you."*

Dear sister, any suffering you're enduring right now is temporary in comparison to our eternity with Christ in Heaven! Be encouraged, and know that He is with you right now and always.

As a Christian, you are never alone. The Holy Spirit is continually

CHAPTER 1: GOD IS OUR REFUGE

within you. God's Spirit indwells you, which means that you are a temple of the Holy Spirit. Please spend some time thinking about that profound and comforting truth.

Reflection Questions:

1. Do you remember to turn to God when your heart is hurting? Why or why not? How can you develop the habit of pouring out your heart to God at the beginning of a painful situation?
2. Which Bible characters who endured pain and suffering do you relate to?
3. Do you find it comforting to remember that Jesus is with you always, even when you can't feel Him or when your faith is momentarily shattered?
4. Which Bible passages comfort you when you're upset?

Chapter 2: When Your Faith is Tested

"For I, the Lord your God, hold your right hand; it is I who say to you, 'Fear not, I am the one who helps you.'" (Isaiah 41:13)

Our sovereign God is holding your hand as you walk through this trial. It's amazing to consider that the Creator of the universe - your Creator - holds your hand.

"So why doesn't He stop this trial that I'm struggling with?" you may wonder. *"Since He's in charge of everything and everyone, why doesn't God fix this situation right now?"*

It's true that God could instantly fix this situation to your liking. Yet, since we know that God loves you, what could be His reasons for allowing you to go through this trial? As our Heavenly Father, what could be the benefit, lesson, or blessings from this situation? Is there some potentially hard-won lesson in this trial that could help you to grow and become more Christ-like? Pray on these questions.

Nobody enjoys going through a trial, despite James exhorting us to "Count it all joy" in James 1:2-4:

"Count it all joy, my brothers, when you meet trials of various kinds, for you know that the testing of your faith produces steadfastness. And let steadfastness have its full effect, that you may be perfect

CHAPTER 2: WHEN YOUR FAITH IS TESTED

and complete, lacking in nothing."

So, is God asking us to throw a party when life turns sour? Not at all! This passage encourages us to approach difficulties with a long-view of the way that trials help us to grow and learn, albeit painfully. In this way, it's joyful to anticipate the valuable lessons and increased endurance that will come out of the trial.

It's helpful to recall past trials that you've endured, to notice what you've learned from these experiences. For example, your priorities may have shifted away from trivial matters. Perhaps the trial helped you to appreciate your loved ones more. Or maybe the situation made you draw closer to God, because self-help options weren't working. Remembering that past difficulties led to blessings can help us to endure our current trials.

The passage in James 1 reminds us that trials can be a testing of your faith. It's easy to proclaim faith in God's sovereignty on sunny days when all is well. But what do we think about God when there's a dark downturn? This is exactly the test that Job went through when he lost everyone and everything at once. Job's faith was being tested, and this may be the case for you as well.

Trials produce *steadfastness* which means the ability to endure, much like an athlete trains to be able to run longer courses. Maybe you can recall a time when you started a new exercise program, and how you gradually built up endurance the more that you practiced. Perhaps God is allowing you to endure this present situation so that you'll be stronger and more filled with faith for the next trial.

Perseverance and steadfastness are developed from the spiritual maturity that comes from enduring trials. Could there be easier ways to develop endurance and maturity? Perhaps, but that's questioning God's direction, isn't it? God obviously believes you can benefit from this situation, or He wouldn't allow you to be in it.

Be encouraged, sister, that God is holding you through this trial. Lean into Him. Pray for Him to increase your faith and to help you to trust that there are blessings from this situation.

God is faithful, even when your faith is being tested. Here's an encouraging passage to help you to focus upon God's mercies in the midst of your struggles:

> *"Because of the Lord's faithful love we do not perish, for His mercies never end. They are new every morning; great is Your faithfulness."* (Lamentations 3:22-23).

The prophet Jeremiah wrote this comforting passage while he was lamenting about the Babylonian exile. Talk about a trial! And yet, Jeremiah kept the faith through it all, and so can we. God's mercies are new every morning.

Reflection Questions:

1. What steps can you take when you feel your faith is flagging?
2. What blessings can you see in retrospect, when you think about trials you've endured in the past?
3. In what ways can you relate to Job's situation of sudden losses?
4. How has pouring your heart out to God helped you to be refreshed when you're going through difficulties?

Chapter 3: The Honor of Suffering

"For you have been called for this purpose, since Christ also suffered for you, leaving you an example for you to follow in His steps, Who committed no sin, nor was any deceit found in His mouth; and while being reviled, He did not revile in return; while suffering, He uttered no threats, but kept entrusting Himself to Him who judges righteously." (1 Peter 2:21-23)

While it may not *feel* like an honor as you endure suffering, the Bible shares important insights and examples about why it's an honor to suffer for Christ's sake. Now, this is not the self-inflicted type of suffering that happens as a result of making unwise choices (which we've all done - no judgment here). This is the type of suffering that accompanies being a Christian, such as losing loved ones who disagree with your Biblical stance, or a job loss, imprisonment, persecution, slander, and so forth because you've shared the Gospel.

Just as our Lord and Savior suffered and died for us, so too are we willing to suffer and die for His sake. In the Sermon on the Mount, Jesus said:

"Blessed are those who are persecuted because of righteousness, for the kingdom

of heaven is theirs. You are blessed when they insult and persecute you and falsely say every kind of evil against you because of me. Be glad and rejoice, because your reward is great in heaven." (Matthew 5:10-12).

We see a clear example when Peter and John were arrested for preaching the Gospel. After they were flogged and released, the apostles rejoiced:

> *"Then they went out from the presence of the Sanhedrin, rejoicing that they were counted worthy to be treated shamefully on behalf of the Name." (Acts 5:41)*

Peter and John saw it as an honor to suffer for Christ's name. How many of us can have this view in the moment of suffering? Perhaps afterward, when we look back we can see it. And of course, this is not to berate us when we're already down. It's more about being encouraged and inspired by the apostles' example. We may not reach their level of trust, yet we can appreciate their example.

In fact, Paul and Barnabas faced severe persecution as they traveled to share the Gospel, including being stoned which is normally an experience leading to death. Yet, despite their hardships, they told the believers who were listening to them:

"It is necessary to go through many hardships to enter the kingdom of God." (Acts 14:22)

What do you think about this statement? It's in the Bible, so we trust that it's divinely inspired truth. Yet, I can recall having the belief (before I was saved) that we could escape earthly troubles if we just stayed positive. Many people sadly hold this belief that they can somehow manipulate God's will to extract blessings. Yet, the Bible clearly states that God is sovereign and in control. It's His will, His way, and His

CHAPTER 3: THE HONOR OF SUFFERING

timing. We're encouraged to express our desires to God in prayer, yet ultimately it's up to Him and we are to trust Him.

Paul and Barnabas emphasized that Christians will face hardships until Jesus returns or calls us home to Heaven. The narrow path is not easy, yet He is with us and uses our difficulties for our growth and His glory. Each time we endure a hardship we come out the other side with refined faith and increased trust and dependence on God.

This recalls the Parable of the Sower (Matthew 13:1-23) in which only the seeds survive and grow which are in good soil, representing those who hear the Gospel and accept it and go on to bear a harvest of fruit for God's kingdom. This is in contrast to the seeds landing on thorns, which represents people who initially claim to believe the Gospel only to later turn away because of worldly cares. Those who are truly saved are able to withstand the storms, because the roots of our faith run deep.

Continuing with our examples of the apostles, one of the most remarkable is when Paul and Silas were thrown into prison. Instead of complaining, they prayed and sang hymns to God while other prisoners listened to them (Acts 16:25). And that's an important point for us to remember: other people are watching what we do in the face of suffering. New Christians and unbelievers will notice how we react to our trials, so it's an important opportunity to share our faith and openly praise God in the storm so that all may hear us give glory to God.

I'm thinking of the Scottish Christian man, John Harper, who went down with the Titanic. As the ship was sinking, Harper swam from person to person in the icy water to share the Gospel with other passengers who were in the water. Harper encouraged them to repent and believe in Jesus Christ.

A survivor of the Titanic testified that Harper swam to him and asked, "Are you saved?" The man replied that he was not, and Harper led him to the Lord right there in the freezing water. The man was rescued and he credited Harper's evangelism with his conversion to Christianity.

Harper perished that night. As he was on the edge of drowning, he selflessly thought of how he could help others in the most important way that there is. After all, Harper knew where his soul was going. What a beautiful loving act of self-sacrifice he displayed. What an inspiration that we can apply to our own lives as we meet people who need to hear about Jesus.

While suffering can feel isolating and overwhelming, there's an honor that comes with it:

> *"And if children, heirs also, heirs of God and fellow heirs with Christ, if indeed we suffer with Him so that we may also be glorified with Him." (Romans 8:17)*

Jesus suffered on our behalf. It's an honor and privilege to suffer for His sake, and to suffer with Him by your side. Philippians 3:10 calls this a "fellowship of His sufferings," in which our trials draw us closer to Christ.

When our earthly resources don't seem to help, we have no choice but to depend completely on God. Talk with Him throughout the day, and tell Him how you feel and what you need. He is there to give you strength and wisdom, dear sister. Remember that you're never alone.

Reflection Questions:

1. Looking back on trials that you've previously endured because of your Christian faith, what blessings can you see that happened as a result?
2. Has there ever been a time when you felt so alone, that God was the only One you felt you could talk to? What was occurring at that time, and have you continued to share your heart with God in

conversations and prayers?
3. In what way do you feel honored to suffer for your Christian faith?
4. How does suffering mold and shape us to be more Christ-like?

Chapter 4: Complaining and Praying

"Do everything without grumbling or arguing, so that you become blameless and pure, children of God without fault in a warped and crooked generation." (Philippians 2:14-15)

As Christians, it's inevitable that we'll go through trials just as our Lord and Savior promised and as He himself endured during His earthly life and death on our behalf. So when the inevitable trials occur, do we handle them by complaining or by pouring our heart out to God in prayer?

Let's look at what the Bible says about complaining. We know that complaining is a natural reaction to pain, and we see this in young children letting their moms know that they're in pain. Complaining as a way of reaching out for help is different than the type of complaining that the Bible addresses.

Complaining, murmuring, and grumbling are the words most often used in the Bible to describe those who have an attitude of ingratitude or distrust in God's reason for allowing the suffering.

The Israelites grumbling in the Exodus that they were better off in Egypt is an example of this type of complaining. They'd forgotten about God's many blessings in literally rescuing them from abusive slavery. They dismissed the fact that God saved their lives during the

CHAPTER 4: COMPLAINING AND PRAYING

first Passover and led them through the Red Sea and away from their pursuers. They minimized God's miraculous provision of water and food during their journey. Instead, they shockingly grumbled against Moses and Aaron: *"If only we had died by the Lord's hand in Egypt!"* (Exodus 16:2-3a).

This type of complaining is probably an immature way of trying to gain God's sympathy, so that He will rescue you. Yet, lashing out at God displays a lack of trust in Him. I love what Job said in the midst of his hardship:

> *"Thou He slay me, yet will I trust Him" (Job 13:15).*

What a statement of trusting God while enduring a crisis! You can pray for God to help you to trust Him more. It's also imperative to study the Bible daily, to gain an understanding of God's character and learn Who He is. After all, it's difficult to trust God if you don't know Him.

Our greatest example of grace during hardship is from our Lord and Savior Jesus, Who suffered greatly and died for our salvation. Yet, Jesus didn't complain, grumble or lash out at His captors, nor did He pray for their destruction. Instead He prayed for our Heavenly Father to forgive them, because they didn't know what they were doing (Luke 23:34).

As followers of Christ, we are called to live as He did:

> *"For you have been called for this purpose, since Christ also suffered for you, leaving you an example for you to follow in His steps, Who committed no sin, nor was any deceit found in His mouth; And while being reviled, He did not revile in return; while suffering, He uttered no threats, but kept entrusting Himself to Him who judges righteously." (1 Peter 2:21-23).*

There's so much to unpack in that passage!

- Jesus suffered for us, leaving an example for us to follow in His steps.
- When He was reviled (which means insulted, criticized or slandered), Jesus didn't revile them in return.
- While He suffered, Jesus didn't utter any threats.
- Throughout His ordeal, Jesus trusted our Heavenly Father.

Jesus didn't complain, grumble, or murmur. Instead He trusted our Heavenly Father. It may seem impossible to reach this level of trust and grace, yet we can pray for Jesus to give us the strength and courage to do so.

Complaining can seem like a cathartic way of releasing our pent-up frustration, but in reality complaining doesn't help. We may believe, like the Israelites in the Exodus, that if we complain enough that someone will feel pity upon us and help us. Yet, how much more effective is it to pray for God's wisdom on how to handle the situation?

Just to be clear, God wants us to pour out our heart to Him in prayer, which includes groaning about our aches, pains, and suffering. The Psalms are a perfect example of how David in the midst of his suffering was transparent with God, such as in Psalm 142:1-2:

> *"I cry aloud to the Lord; I lift up my voice to the Lord for mercy. I pour out before him my complaint; before him I tell my trouble."*

David openly shared his complaints with God, yet it was always to ask for God's help. The key is that David never directed his complaints against God's will. In the storms, David always praised God.

Similarly, the weeping prophet Jeremiah spoke candidly to God about his grief and anguish over Jerusalem's destruction. Yet Jeremiah never criticized God's plans.

There's also the prophet Habakkuk who brought his complaints

CHAPTER 4: COMPLAINING AND PRAYING

before God, while simultaneously acknowledging God's sovereignty. Habakkuk was struggling to understand why God allowed injustice to persist. Yet, Haakkuk's complaints were about seeking answers, not in questioning God's authority.

These Biblical examples show that it's acceptable to bring our complaints before God, as long as we do so with trust and reverence for God. The Bible's admonitions about complaining are about grumbling with bitterness, or questioning God's wisdom.

Even in our darkest moments, we need to remember the promise of Romans 8:28:

> *"And we know that in all things God works for the good of those who love him, who have been called according to his purpose."*

I pray that you trust in the Lord, dear sister, and that you trust that He's working out your life for good - even when His plan doesn't seem clear or like the plan that you would choose.

Reflection Questions:

1. What's the main difference between David's complaints in the Psalms, and the Israelites' complaints in the wilderness?
2. Have you poured out your heart to God, including telling Him about your complaints, while simultaneously trusting and praising Him?
3. How does daily Bible study help us to trust God more?
4. Do you ever find it difficult to ask others for help? What are some ways to directly ask others for help, so that they know you really need assistance?

Chapter 5: Momentary Light Affliction

"For our momentary light affliction is producing for us an absolutely incomparable eternal weight of glory." (2 Corinthians 4:17)

The encouraging verse that opens this chapter reminds us that our suffering in this world - while very real and very painful - are temporary and serve a greater purpose in God's loving hands. As Christian women, we're called to fix our eyes upon the glory and hope of eternal life in Christ.

The "momentary light affliction" in this verse isn't trying to minimize what you're currently enduring, but to remind you that it isn't forever. Your suffering will end, dear sister. And as a believer, what awaits you in incomparable to anything here on earth. Even our best days will pale beside what awaits us in Heaven.

Notice how this verse contrasts *momentary light* with *eternal weight*. Momentary means temporary, while eternal means forever. Light means that earthly afflictions can feel overwhelming in the moment, yet the suffering is relatively minor compared to the glory that's to come. *Weight* means that our eternity is immense and *of great worth*. Our momentary light afflictions are producing for us an incomparable eternal weight of glory.

CHAPTER 5: MOMENTARY LIGHT AFFLICTION

This isn't about wishing that our earthly life would finish soon, though. As long as we're breathing, God has a plan and purpose for us. Whether it's sharing the Gospel, or learning how to draw nearer to God through our suffering, there's a reason that you're still here on earth. And when it's your time to go, according to God's will and timing, you'll be with Christ where there's no more tears, grief, crying, death, or pain (Revelation 21:4).

When Paul suffered through persecution and imprisonment, he wrote this encouraging reminder:

> *"I consider that our present sufferings are not worth comparing with the glory that will be revealed in us." (Romans 8:18)*

What an inspiring reminder that our memories of suffering will fall away when Jesus lifts us up to Heaven! Although our suffering seems to last for a long time here on earth, it's a relatively short amount of time through the lens of eternity.

The blessings which we receive right here in this lifetime are often products of suffering. Our biggest blessing of course is our salvation. God in His infinite mercy and grace chose to save us out of darkness and He gave us a new life and a new heart!

Some falsely teach that once we become a Christian, all of our troubles fall away. They twist Scripture to claim that Jesus will bring them health, wealth, and a job promotion. Yet, Jesus promised that in this world we would have trouble (John 16:33), but that we should take heart because He overcame the world:

> *"I have told you these things, so that in me you may have peace. In this world you will have trouble. But take heart! I have overcome the world."*

Jesus never sugarcoated what life is like for His disciples. He acknowledged that trouble and suffering are inevitable for Christians, including persecution, sickness, and personal loss. We aren't promised a life without hardship, but we are promised access to God's strength to endure hardships. He also promises to be with us through our trials.

When Jesus said, *"In Me you may have peace,"* He was reminding us that peace doesn't come from the world, but from abiding in Him. It's a peace that comes from knowing that no matter what happens in this world, believers are held by Christ.

When Jesus said *"In this world you will have trouble,"* He was being kind by telling us the truth that this is a fallen world filled with sinners, many of whom hate Christians. Trials are a part of earthly life for believers.

When Jesus said, *"But take heart! I have overcome the world,"* He was assuring us of His victory. Believers can stand firm in the face of adversity since Jesus defeated sin and the devil. God is more powerful than any troubles we may face. Jesus' words encourage us to endure hardships, once we realize that *all* Christians face struggles, and we can all find hope in His victory.

Reflection Questions:

1. Does it encourage you to know that all Christians face adversity and that you're not alone in your suffering?
2. How can you keep a focus of hope and assurance of living with Christ in eternity where they'll be no more suffering?
3. When you're in a painful moment, what are some ways to keep your thoughts upon Jesus?
4. How do we have peace in Jesus, when our lives and bodies aren't at peace? Is His peace different than the world's definition of peace?

Chapter 6: God's Refining Process

> *"Dear Friends, don't be surprised when the firey ordeal comes among you to test you, as if something unusual were happening to you. Instead, rejoice as you share in the sufferings of Christ, so that you may also rejoice with great joy when His glory is revealed."* (1 Peter 4:12-13).

The Apostle Peter through the Holy Spirit's inspiration reminds us to not be caught off guard when trials occur. Hardships are the usual, not the unusual, for believers.

This passage describes a "firey ordeal," which brings to mind how precious metals are refined in fire. The heat brings the impurities to the surface, so that the metal can be refined and purified. In the same way, firey trials - though admittedly painful and unpleasant - are part of our sanctification process of refinement. God uses our suffering to purify our faith, so that we're looking to Him for help, and not to our own selves.

Anyone who says that God is guaranteed to heal a person's illness or bring them prosperity, is speaking falsely and unbiblically. The only guarantee is that Christians will face adversity, and that God will be there with them through the trial. Unfortunately, those who listen to the false prosperity gospel will be surprised when they experience firey ordeals.

It's not *whether* we'll experience trials, but *how* we deal with them that matters. If we turn to God with praise and trust, our ordeal won't upset us to the degree that it would if we held a false belief about what Christian life looks like.

This passage reminds us that trials come to test us. In the King James Bible, the word *try* is used, in the same meaning as *test*. The Biblical Koine Greek word for try or test (*peirasmō*) usually means a process which reveals the quality of something. It can also mean a trial that reveals a person's character and values. So, the trial of suffering can demonstrate the authenticity and strength of the believer's faith. This means that suffering acts as a divine instrument of refinement.

The Bible frequently describes precious metals being refined in fire to illustrate that people are refined by firey ordeals, such as these verses:

> *"He will sit as a refiner and purifier of silver; He will purify the sons of Levi and purge them as gold and silver, that they may offer to the Lord an offering in righteousness." (Malachi 3:3).*

And in 1 Peter 1:6-7, God said that we're more precious than gold that perishes though it is tested by fire. This passage explains that we go through firey ordeals to test the genuineness of our faith. If our faith isn't genuine, we'll walk away from the Gospel and decide that suffering for Christ isn't worth it. In cases like that, the faith was probably never genuine in the first place.

Doesn't that remind you of Christ's followers who fell away when He made some hard statements? These followers just wanted to be fed physical food, not spiritual food. The moment when discipleship got tough, they disappeared (c.f., John 6:60-66). Jesus even confronted them: "Yet there are some of you who do not believe." Jesus had known from the beginning which of them did not believe and who would betray

CHAPTER 6: GOD'S REFINING PROCESS

Him (John 6:64).

The prophet Isaiah recorded God saying, "Behold, I have refined you, but not as silver; I have tested you in the furnace of affliction." (Isaiah 48:10). So, as we're enduring seasons of struggle, let's keep in mind that this is God's refinement and testing of our faith that we're experiencing. As Proverbs 17:3 says:

> *"The refining pot is for silver and the furnace for gold, but the Lord tests the hearts."*

Suffering in the Christian life isn't random or meaningless, dear sister. God is sovereign and every aspect of life is under His direction. Trials are God's purposeful tool that He uses to refine believers, test our commitment and faith, and to steer us to trust Him.

Reflection Questions:

1. Can you think of any impurities (such as distrust or willfulness, etc.) that God may have brought to the surface for refining, as a result of trials you've endured?
2. Please find and watch a video that shows the process of precious metals being refined and purified in fire? How does this video relate to the process you've gone through during seasons of struggles?
3. Please read John 6:60-66. When you think about Jesus' followers who walked away from Him, what comes to your mind about their priorities?
4. Have you ever been falsely told that becoming a Christian means that you'll have a problem-free life, or that you attracted problems with your thoughts? What do you think about these sort of teachings now?

Chapter 7: Jesus our Lighthouse and Anchor

Lighthouses are beautiful symbols of resilient light in the midst of a storm, and for this reason Jesus is often referred to as a Lighthouse. It's not a biblical term, yet it describes Him perfectly.

Jesus Himself said:

> *"I am the light of the world. He who follows Me shall not walk in darkness, but have the light of life." (John 8:12)*

Just as a lighthouse shines light in the darkness for protection and guidance, so too does Jesus illuminate our path so that we don't walk in darkness. You can probably think back to your life prior to salvation where you tried to control everything by yourself. Yet, as followers of Jesus, we rest in His strength and wisdom.

As Christians, we encounter frightening moments when life feels like an unpredictable and tumultuous ocean tossing us around. Remember when the disciples were caught in a storm on the Sea of Galilee? Jesus appeared to them, walking upon the water which terrified the disciples even more. And what did Jesus say to them for reassurance?

> *"Be of good cheer! It is I; do not be afraid." (Matthew 14:27)*

CHAPTER 7: JESUS OUR LIGHTHOUSE AND ANCHOR

Jesus gives us comfort and encouragement during our storms in life. Hebrews 6:19 also tells us that Jesus is the anchor of our souls Who provides stability and security when life seems chaotic:

> *"This hope we have as an anchor of the soul both sure and steadfast, and which enters the Presence behind the veil."*

Have you ever been on a ship that used an anchor to stay in one place in the open sea? It's remarkable that this one piece of metal with a long rope or chain can hold a ship steady against waves and currents, yet anchors hold the ship securely in place. In the same way, lighthouses are designed to withstand the fiercest storms and harshest conditions.

Jesus, like a lighthouse and anchor, holds us secure during life's storms. Now, this doesn't mean that Jesus will instantly fix everything according to your liking. It means that He's there with you during the storm. As you turn to Jesus during your struggles, He gives you direction and assurance.

Notice how Revelation 21:23 describes Jesus' light:

> *"The city had no need of the sun or of the moon to shine in it, for the glory of God illuminated it. The Lamb is its light."*

Jesus' light is brighter than the sun or the moon, because He is the light of the world. So, when your world seems darkened with troubles and you aren't sure what to do, turn to Jesus to light your path with His wisdom, love, and encouragement. Read the Gospels, pray, and keep your thoughts firmly anchored on Him.

Reflection Questions:

1. Can you think of a time when you were frightened, but then you

remembered to pray? How did praying lift you out of the darkness?
2. When you think of Jesus as your lighthouse, what comes to mind? How does this reassure and comfort you?
3. Has your home's power ever turned off during a storm? In what ways is turning to Jesus similar to having your electricity and lights restored?
4. In what ways does Jesus help to anchor you when you're frightened?

Chapter 8: His Grace is Sufficient

"But He has said to me, 'My grace is sufficient for you, for power is perfected in weakness.' Most gladly, therefore, I will rather boast about my weaknesses, so that the power of Christ may dwell in me." (2 Corinthians 12:9)

Where did we women get the idea that we need to be the strong ones who have it all together? Of course, we're responsible for our family and we're active members of our local church. Yet, how many times do we push ourselves to exhaustion by juggling way too many responsibilities? How often do we judge ourselves for feeling like a hot mess, instead of our idea of what a Christian woman "should be"? Do we negatively compare ourselves to the women at church who seem to have it all together?

The context of 2 Corinthians 12:9 passage is Paul being criticized and unfavorably compared to "super apostles" who boasted of their spiritual gifts and accomplishments. Instead of trying to one-up them or defend himself, Paul boasts about his weakness and glorifies Christ.

Paul also said that a "thorn in the flesh" was keeping him humble (2 Corinthians 12:7). We don't know what that thorn specifically was, except for Paul calling it a "messenger of Satan." Theologians have speculated what the thorn was, yet unless the Bible describes something, we shouldn't venture into guesses. What we do know for certain is that Paul was describing a difficulty, and he emphasized that God's grace was sufficient.

God's grace is the unmerited favor that God gave to us when He forgave our sins through Jesus' shed blood on the cross. We didn't earn our salvation; it was a free gift by God's grace and mercy. Paul was a highly educated Pharisee who'd previously persecuted Christians to death. After God saved Paul's soul, he was understandably humbled. Paul realized that his earthly accomplishments were worthless in comparison to what God's grace had bestowed upon him.

God's grace removes the just penalty for our sins, but grace doesn't remove suffering or the consequences of our past sins. Grace also enables us to endure and persevere in the midst of suffering. In our weakness, God's power is most fully manifested. In other words, we can't do anything in our own strength, but only in God's strength.

Jesus' victory over sin and death happened in the moment of His death, which to the world, would appear as weakness. Through His sacrifice, Jesus achieved the greatest victory of all.

In 2 Corinthians 12:10, Paul said, *"For when I am weak, then I am strong."* It's through humility and admitting our need for help and especially our need for Jesus as our Savior, that we depend upon God instead of upon ourselves.

Although the world idolizes self-sufficiency and has mottos like, "You've got the power," we Christians are called to a different standard. When we're most vulnerable and humble, that's when God is most glorified. In our brokenness, our need for God's power is the most clear.

So, when Paul said that he'd rather boast about his weakness so that the power of Christ would dwell in him (c.f., 2 Corinthians 12:9b), we learn an important lesson: We see God's power in our most vulnerable times. When we're broken, shredded, overwhelmed, and just feel done

CHAPTER 8: HIS GRACE IS SUFFICIENT

with everything, that's when we can know God's power even more. We are encouraged by His strength!

God doesn't ask you to be a superwoman when life is overwhelming. In fact, relying upon our own strength to be superwoman is the opposite of what God wants for us. We're called to lean into God and rely upon Him instead of upon ourselves, as 2 Corinthians 1:8-9 reminds us:

"For we do not want you to be unaware, brothers, of the affliction we experienced in Asia. For we were so utterly burdened beyond our strength that we despaired of life itself. Indeed, we felt that we had received the sentence of death. But that was to make us rely not on ourselves but on God who raises the dead."

This passage emphasizes that in times of suffering, God is drawing us nearer to Himself. This points to the importance of relying upon God instead of trying to draw from our own strength.

When you're feeling overwhelmed and juggling too much, don't try to power through it dear sister. Instead, that's the time to pray for God's wisdom and strength.

Reflection Questions:

1. What influences have led to any self-reliant characteristics that you may have? How can you be more reliant upon God and less upon yourself?
2. Are you dealing with any fears about being judged if you present yourself as weak and needing help? How can you overcome these fears?
3. Can you think of a time when you cried out to God for strength, and He lifted you up? What was that like for you?
4. In what way is God glorified when we turn to Him, instead of trying to do everything ourselves?

Chapter 9: Hope in the Midst of Suffering

"Through the Lord's mercies we are not consumed, because His compassions fail not. They are new every morning; great is your faithfulness." (Lamentations 3:22-23)

The prophet Jeremiah wrote these words through the inspiration of the Holy Spirit, at a time when Jeremiah was devastated over Jerusalem's destruction and the Babylonian exile.

It was an era of suffering when God's judgment came to pass, after people ignored the warnings that Jeremiah and other prophets repeatedly gave to them. Instead of repenting, the people continued in their idolatry and they were sent away for 70 years to Babylon. The Temple and the city were destroyed, and most of the people were hauled into captivity. In the midst of this devastation and while writing his divinely inspired laments, Jeremiah praised God for His mercy and faithfulness.

The Bible has many encouraging examples where the light of hopefulness shines through the darkness of despair. May we also remember to praise God in the storms of life! Not just mouthing the words of praise. Not trying to persuade God with our praises. Our praises need to be heartfelt and sincere, without conditions attached. God is great because

CHAPTER 9: HOPE IN THE MIDST OF SUFFERING

He is great - regardless of whether or not He grants our prayers as we would like Him to.

The Apostle Paul also praised God in the midst of suffering. One example is when Paul was imprisoned and yet he wrote this hopeful passage in Philippians 4:6-7:

> *"Be anxious for nothing, but in everything by prayer and supplication, with thanksgiving, let your requests be made know to God; and the peace of God, which surpasses all understanding, will guard your hearts and minds through Christ Jesus."*

Here he was under the threat of capital punishment in a dank Roman prison, writing an encouraging note for all believers! These words under the Holy Spirit's inspiration must have comforted Paul with the reminder to pray instead of being anxious.

Another example is when the apostles were singing hymns and praising God from their jail cells (Acts 16:25-26). Their acts of worship were witnessed by other prisoners, as well.

The ultimate example of hope during suffering is found in our Lord and Savior Jesus Christ, who endured excruciating suffering on our behalf. Yet, Jesus continued to praise His Father throughout His ordeal, as described in Hebrews 12:2:

> *"Looking unto Jesus, the author and finisher of our faith, who for the joy that was set before Him endured the cross, despising the shame, and has sat down at the right hand of the throne of God."*

We also see Job praising God after he'd lost his health, finances, and children. Despite being in so much pain and despair, Job proclaimed his faith under the Holy Spirit's inspiration:

"For I know that my Redeemer lives, and He shall stand at last on the earth; and after my skin is destroyed, this I know, that in my flesh I shall see God, Whom I shall see for myself, and my eyes shall behold, and not another. How my heart years within me!" (Job 19:25-27)

In the midst of his suffering, Job held onto hope that his Redeemer lives and that one day he would behold God. Instead of focusing upon his present misery, Job focused upon the glory to come. We are blessed to be on this side of the cross, and to know our Redeemer is Jesus!

This isn't to diminish the very real suffering you may be experiencing right now, but instead to encourage you to keep your eyes fixed upon Jesus. He is our only hope and light in this dark and fallen world.

Of course, King David is another example of someone who praised God in the middle of his ordeals. David's psalms frequently expressed his faith in the Lord, as well as his prayers for God's help. Throughout the Bible, we see examples of praising God during times of deep suffering.

Have you ever seen a flower sprouting through a crack in the pavement, representing God's glorious creation overcoming adversity? Isaiah 61:3 captures this growth that can result from seasons of struggle:

"To console those who mourn in Zion,
To give them beauty for ashes,
The oil of joy for mourning,
The garment of praise for the spirit of heaviness;
That they may be called trees of righteousness,
The planting of the LORD, that He may be glorified."

This passage summarizes the hope of renewal that God offers to us. There's a future restoration, with today's pain giving way to tomorrow's glory in Christ. Be encouraged, dear sister! As long as you've put your

CHAPTER 9: HOPE IN THE MIDST OF SUFFERING

trust in Jesus, you can be certain that He's holding your hand through your trials. Our hope is rooted and grounded in God's promises in His Word. We can confidently trust God's promises and know that His mercies are indeed new every morning.

Reflection Questions:

1. What are some triggers that you can avoid, that tend to make you feel discouraged?
2. How does reading the Bible daily help to keep you focused upon Jesus?
3. Are you inspired by these examples of praising God and proclaiming faith in the midst of suffering? In what ways can you model after these examples?
4. How does praying help to increase your gratitude and appreciation for God?

Chapter 10: Uplifted with Hope

"Why are you cast down, O my soul, and why are you in turmoil within me? Hope in God; for I shall again praise him, my salvation." (Psalm 42:5)

I love how the Psalms acknowledge our most vulnerable and tender feelings. In one breath the Psalmists describe their darkest thoughts, and in the next breath they praise God as our source of hope. Psalm 42:5 reminds us that being "cast down" is an inner struggle that can be uplifted when we shift our focus from self to God for comfort.

Let's discuss the inner struggle that can sometimes worsen our suffering, and how we can remember to turn to God instead. There's this cycle that most don't want to acknowledge, because it's kind of embarrassing. As I discuss this cycle, please know that I'm not judging anyone because I've been there, done that myself.

This is a cycle of pushing away hope and encouragement and instead wallowing in self-pity. Again, no judgment here. We can feel so overwhelmed that we retreat into ourselves because it feels familiar to pity ourselves. It's like we're going into a private "safe space" where no one understands how we feel, except ourselves. When this happens, we may forget to pray or to read our Bible. We may push away well-meaning people. It's the emotional equivalent of making a blanket fort.

Sometimes this cycle is related to secondary gains if we receive a reward of sympathy or nicer treatment from others, which makes us feel loved and understood. It's great when others care for us. The problem comes when someone prefers the sympathy over turning to God to lift them out of despair.

For others, self-pity can be a way to avoid work or other responsibilities. Of course, there are people who genuinely are unable to work because of their disabilities. This is about those who remain in an emotionally and mentally defeated state, rather than turning to God for encouragement.

This cycle can also be a defense mechanism against further emotional pain. Self-pity becomes a shield to protect us from further hurt when we decide not to get our hopes up, so we won't be disappointed. Putting up walls to avoid being hurt also leads to loneliness.

Praise Jesus for extending His hand to us for comfort and rest, as He said in Matthew 11:28-30:

> *"Come to me, all you who are weary and burdened and I will give you rest. Take my yoke upon you and learn from me, for I am gentle and humble in heart, and you will find rest for your souls."*

Jesus is our source of hope, encouragement, and comfort to bring us out of the darkness of self-pity and despair. Even if you're in a situation that seems hopeless, pray for God's help. You may not see a way out, but God can. Of course, God isn't a magical genie who grants our wishes. His answer to your prayers may look different than your expectations. Yet, His way is always the best:

"We know that in all things God works for the good of those who love him, who have been called according to his purpose." (Romans 8:28)

Even in the midst of turmoil, God is in charge. He is sovereign over everyone and everything, and He transforms situations and people for good and His glory. Reach out to Him in prayer right now, dear sister. Pour out your heart to Him. Praise Him from your heart. Ask Him for help, including that He lift you up and fill you with hope.

Reflection Questions:

1. Have you ever wallowed in self-pity? What was that like? Was it helpful? When you reflect upon any reasons for staying in self-pity, what do you get?
2. Have you ever pushed away help from someone who seemed well-meaning? Why and would you do that again these days?
3. How does it feel to consider that Jesus is offering rest to weary believers?
4. Can you think of examples where God turned a terrible situation around, and ultimately used it for good and His glory?

Chapter 11: Count it All Joy

"Count it all joy, my brothers, when you meet trials of various kinds, for you know that the testing of your faith produces steadfastness. And let steadfastness have its full effect, that you may be perfect and complete, lacking in nothing." (James 1:2-4)

Whenever I'm going through a challenge, I play a Bible audio of the book of James. The moment that I hear the narrator say, "Count it all joy," I feel comforted, and my focus is redirected from pessimism to hope.

I'll admit that joy is the last thing I feel when I'm faced with hardship. Yet, the encouragement of this passage is uplifting because it's a reminder that our suffering has purpose and meaning. It's like the exertion of exercising in exchange for better health. We may not enjoy the exercise in the moment, but afterward we're glad that we did the workout. I'm not trying minimizing any sorrow you're experiencing. I've been there, too! This is just shifting our perspective to see the blessings within the messiness.

James 1:2 calls us to *"count it all joy."* Perhaps we don't feel joyful about the circumstances, but we can have joy knowing that God is using our trial to grow us according to His will.

This passage from our God-breathed inerrant Bible says that when we meet different types of trials, it's a testing of our faith that produces perseverance. Again, with our exercising metaphor: the more we workout, the fitter we become.

The Bible talks a lot about the importance of perseverance. For example, Romans 5:3-5 says that we rejoice in suffering because it produces endurance, and endurance produces character, which produces hope because God's love has been poured into our hearts through the Holy Spirit who has been given to us.

As our endurance increases, we're better equipped to view new trials with faith and trust in God. This gives us hope and encouragement to keep going when we're in the midst of a challenge.

Hebrews 10:36 discusses our need for endurance so we can fulfill the will of God and receive what is promised. Similarly, Philippians 3:14 talks about pressing on for the prize of the upward call of God in Christ Jesus.

God uses our suffering to build our character and endurance. Every trial has a purpose. We may not understand God's reasoning, yet He's the One in charge, not us. The word "steadfastness" is sometimes interpreted as "patience," and our trials call for us to patiently wait upon God's timing and will. Patience is a part of trusting in the Lord, even if we can't see evidence that our prayers have been heard. James 5:10 cites the Biblical prophets as an example of those who remained patient while suffering.

The book of James continues to encourage us with this verse:

> *"Blessed is the man who remains steadfast under trial, for when he has stood the test he will receive the crown of life, which God has promised to those who love him." (James 1:12)*

This verse highlights "steadfast," to emphasize the importance of and the rewards for our perseverance under trial. James 5:11 says, *"we consider those blessed who remained steadfast"* and then gives Job as an example of steadfastness.

We don't need to draw upon our own strength to persevere. In fact, we *can't* because our human strength is too weak to withstand trials on its own. We need Christ's strength to endure, and this means turning to Him in prayer and asking Him to lift us up.

Pray for God to strengthen you, and don't try to do anything on your own dear sister. When we feel weak or discouraged, that's the time to pray for God's strength to carry us through. Remember that Jesus promised to be with us always.

Reflection Questions:

1. What blessings can you count from a trial that you went through? Does it bring you joy to count those blessings?
2. How can we remember to turn to Christ for strength, instead of trying to draw upon our human strength?
3. Can you recall a trial you went through, where your perseverance obviously came from God because no human could have endured it on their own?
4. In what ways have your struggles increased your steadfastness, so that you're better equipped for new trials?

Chapter 12: Cast Your Cares on Him

"casting all your anxiety on Him, because He cares for you." (1 Peter 5:7)

Anxiety robs us of peace and joy, because it conjures up a sense that something awful is about to happen. When we're anxious, we may isolate or try to control everything as a way of coping with the fear and nervousness. We may even engage in unhealthful behaviors to try to reduce anxiety. Praise God for giving us instructions in His Word about how to deal with anxiety!

In 1 Peter 5:7, we're instructed to cast our anxiety on God. What a comforting thought to give our worries to God! And this verse is much more than "giving" our worries, as the original Koine Greek word *casting* is transliterated *epirrhiptō*, meaning to throw upon. Think of a skilled fisherman casting his line far out into the water, as an example. This is the kind of thrust that God wants you to use with casting your anxiety on Him.

Take the heavy burdens from your heart and toss them to God. He knows that you care about everyone involved in this situation, so He's not asking you to stop caring. There's a big difference between *caring* about a situation and the people involved, and *carrying* a burden. Cast your burden and anxieties to God. Don't carry them, sweet sister! Give them to God.

Which brings us to the second part of this verse, "because He cares for you." This is the reason why God wants us to cast our anxieties to Him. The word *cares* is derived from the Greek word transliterated *melō*, which means to being concerned about someone in a personal way with compassion. This isn't a detached or distant form of caring. This is your Creator Who knows you, caring for you and being actively involved in your life.

Under the inspiration of the Holy Spirit, the apostle Peter wrote this verse to Christians who were suffering persecution and hardships because of their faith. 1 Peter 5:7 is an encouragement and reminder to trust God, instead of trying to resolve the trials on our own strength. It's a call to give our burdens to God and trust that He's sovereignly in control.

If you're struggling to cast your anxieties upon God, please take those struggles to God. Admit any fears you may have about giving Him your anxiety, such as control or trust issues. Ask Him for help with *everything*, including learning how to trust Him and how to let go of the desire to be in control.

As anxieties arise, casting them to God is an act of faith in Him and an acknowledgment of our human limitations. When you're aware of being anxious, stop and pour out your heart to God. Tell him about every thought and worry. He already knows what's in your heart, and when you share it with Him you'll know that He's in charge. Pray for God to give you peace, assurance, comfort, strength, and wisdom. Rest in His timing and His will, because God answers prayers in ways that differ from our expectations.

As Psalm 55:22 reminds us:

> *"Cast your burden upon the Lord and He will sustain you; He will never allow the righteous to be shaken."*

As you cast your burdens and anxieties to God, you may not see an immediate change in your circumstances, yet you likely will feel an immediate sense of relief. Trust in Him, dear sister, and give Him your cares.

Reflection Questions:

1. Do you have any control issues that you're aware of, that make you hesitate asking God for help? Have you asked God to help you to trust Him more?
2. When you think of casting your anxieties on God, what comes to mind?
3. In what ways have you tried to reduce anxiety in the past? How did those methods affect you?
4. Have you prayed for God to help you to have patience with His timing? In what ways could this prayer comfort you?

Chapter 13: Thy Will be Done

> "And He went a little beyond them, and fell on His face and prayed, saying, 'My Father, if it is possible, let this cup pass from Me; yet not as I will, but as You will." (Matthew 26:39)

Do you have willful tendencies? Probably all of us are willful to a degree. Willfulness means that we get an idea in our head about what we want, and we expect everyone - including God - to go along with our idea. Yet, we all know that God's will is filled with omniscient wisdom. He sees all and knows all.

Remember when the prophet Jonah was called by God to preach to Nineveh, and Jonah rebelled by boarding a ship in the wrong direction? Sadly, Jonah's rebellion affected the others on the ship, as God sent a storm to direct Jonah back on course.

Finally, after being thrown overboard and swallowed by a great fish, Jonah repented and obeyed God. Jonah's story can apply to us when God sends storms that are ultimately to humble us into obeying God. It's a painful lesson at the time, yet when we look back after awhile, we can see God's wisdom, love, and sovereignty in it all.

This reminds me of Isaiah 30:20-21 which says, "The Lord gives you the bread of adversity and the water of affliction." God can send and allow us to struggle as He directs our path. During these struggles, God is with you dear sister.

The three Persons of the Holy Trinity: the Father, the Son, and the Holy Spirit are all co-equal and co-eternal. None are superior or older than another in the Holy Trinity. During Jesus' earthly ministry, He was *temporarily* subordinate to the Father. Philippians 2:5-8 explains that Jesus willingly humbled or emptied himself, during His earthly ministry. During that time, Jesus chose to not live in the fullness of His position, divine majesty or omnipotence, but instead submitted to the will of the Father. Jesus voluntarily did this so that He could sacrifice Himself to save us from the wrath for the sins we've all committed (Romans 5:8). *That's love!*

Jesus gave us the ultimate example of submitting to God's will in the Garden of Gethsemane as He was about to be crucified. Jesus knew what torture this would involve, and since He was both fully God *and* fully man, He was about to feel excruciating pain. So, He prayed whether it was possible for the cup of suffering to pass Him by. And then Jesus prayed the most humble prayer that we should all model after: *"Yet not as I will, but as You will"* (Matthew 26:39). Jesus was ready to suffer and die according to His Father's will.

The Koine Greek word for will in this verse is *thelō ethelō*, which means inclination or desire. Jesus expressed His human desire to avoid the suffering of scourging and crucifixion. Yet, He ultimately submitted to the Father's plan of redemption through Jesus' sacrifice to save us. Jesus chose obedience to the Father over His own preferences.

Some teachers falsely claim that if we're obedient to God, all our cares will disappear (these are usually the same teachers who falsely say that we need to offer them seed-money in order to reap God's bounty). Yet, Jesus' own example shows that obedience leads to God's will being done, and has nothing to do with achieving our own creature comforts. Suffering may continue while we submit to God.

It's important to pray for God to give you the strength to be in

CHAPTER 13: THY WILL BE DONE

submission and obedience to Him. We shouldn't try to do anything in our strength, but always praying for God's strength to help us.

Romans 12:1-2 instructs us about being submissive to God's will:

> *"Therefore I urge you, brethren, by the mercies of God, to present your bodies a living and holy sacrifice, acceptable to God, which is your spiritual service of worship. And do not be conformed to this world, but be transformed by the renewing of your mind, so that you may prove what the will of God is, that which is good and acceptable and perfect."*

In the phrase "present your bodies" in this passage, the word *present* in the original Koine Greek is *parastanō*, which means to voluntarily offer something. So, presenting your bodies as a living sacrifice means to volunteer that God would use you for His glory.

Notice also that this passage emphasizes submitting to God instead of conforming to the world. Oh, the pressures can be strong to conform to the world's styles and fads! Yet, this passage says that we will be transformed (changed for the better) by renewing our mind. Ephesians 5:26 says that we're cleansed by the washing of water with God's Word. Studying the Bible is cleansing and transformative.

In other words, when we shift from insisting upon our own will (which is usually influenced by the world), and instead desire what God desires, we are following God's will which is always good, acceptable, and perfect.

Dear sister, let's remember that God's plans are far beyond our limited human understanding, as the Lord declared to the prophet Isaiah:

> *"'For my thoughts are not your thoughts,*
> *Nor are your ways My ways," declares the Lord.*
> *"For as the heavens are higher than the earth,*

*So are My ways higher than your ways
And My thoughts than your thoughts."* (Isaiah 55:8-9)

The Hebrew word for thoughts in this passage, תוֹבָשְׁחַמ (*machashebeth*), which means *plans* or *intentions*, emphasizes that God's plans and intentions are far beyond our own. This realization should lead to awe at these two attributes of God:

- **God's transcendence**, which means that He is completely beyond, independent of, separate from, and above His creations (including us). He is great, mighty, and majestic.
- **God's immanence** means that He is actively involved in the world, despite His transcendence. God is separate from His creation, yet He isn't distant or detached.

God is both beyond creation (transcendent) and simultaneously He's actively involved in His creation (immanent).

These two attributes are comforting as we endure hardships, to know that we serve an extraordinary God and He is there for us, as Psalm 145:18 illustrates:

"The Lord is near to all who call on him, to all who call on him in truth."

We can know God's will by studying the Bible daily, praying for God's will to be done, and by talking to biblically solid mature Christians such as our pastor, church elders, or our Bible study teacher. We know that God would never ask us to do anything that would contradict what He's said in the Bible. Even in the midst of hardship, we can trust that God's will for us is the best (and really the only) way.

CHAPTER 13: THY WILL BE DONE

Reflection Questions:

1. When you think back about times in your life when you may have been willful, how did that work out? What did you learn from those situations?
2. Do you trust that God's will is far superior to your own?
3. In the midst of suffering, are you praying for God to give you the strength to surrender your own will for His?
4. How does Jesus' prayer at the Garden of Gethsemane for His Father's will affect your decisions to turn to God's will?

Chapter 14: Blessings Out of Adversity

"But as for you, you meant evil against me; but God meant it for good, in order to bring it about as it is this day, to save many people alive." (Genesis 50:20)

In this verse, Joseph acknowledges that his brothers acted in evil ways when they'd sold him into slavery. Yet, despite their diabolical plot, God used the situation for good as Joseph became a high-ranking Egyptian official who stored food. When a famine arose, the Israelites (including Joseph's family) were able to eat because of Joseph's foresight.

When Joseph's brothers came to Egypt to buy food, they discovered that Joseph was still alive and that he was an official. The brothers were terrified of receiving a well-deserved punishment from Joseph, yet God was glorified instead.

This verse emphasizes that an evil plan by men has no power in the face of God's plan for good. Joseph went through horrible ordeals before he was elevated into the Pharaoh's court. Joseph was left for dead, sold into slavery, falsely accused of adultery, and imprisoned. Yet, through that adversity, God was shaping Joseph and the situation to preserve many lives.

It's the same with our adversities, dear sister. God knows what

CHAPTER 14: BLESSINGS OUT OF ADVERSITY

you're going through and what you're facing. If, like Joseph, you've been betrayed by people God knows this, too. God isn't passive in our suffering. He hears our cries and our prayers.

We've looked at this verse before, because it's so pivotal for our encouragement in the midst of trials:

> *"And we know that all things work together for good to those who love God, to those who are called according to His purpose."* (Romans 8:28)

God can bring good out of every situation, no matter how difficult the circumstances. Whether it's drawing people closer to God, increasing their spiritual growth, or putting someone in the right place to help others, God is sovereign over everyone and everything and it's always for good.

God's plan often differs from what we imagine would be the best solution, so our prayers also need to be that we would appreciate God's blessings - even if they're not what we expected. We can pray to have more appreciation and gratitude for God.

Joseph's story is encouraging because it's a testimony of God's faithfulness. We can rest on God's promise that in our darkest hours He is there with us. God can bring blessings out of adversity in ways we could never imagine. Often we recognize these hard-won blessings after time has passed, when we can look back and see the bigger picture and the connections. In the meantime, may we trust in God's goodness.

Reflection Questions:

1. Thinking back to challenges you've endured, how have you seen God's workmanship bringing about blessings from those situations?

2. How can you increase your trust in God's sovereignty when faced with hardship?
3. When we look at Joseph forgiving his brothers, does this remind you that there's someone you need to forgive? Have you prayed for God to help you to forgive?
4. How does expecting God to bring goodness out of adversity, help your mindset about the situation?

Chapter 15: More Than Conquerors

"Who can separate us from the love of Christ? Can affliction or distress or persecution or famine or nakedness or danger or sword? As it is written: Because of you we are being put to death all day long; we are counted as sheep to be slaughtered. No, in all these things we are more than conquerors through him who loved us. For I am persuaded that neither death nor life, angels nor rulers, things present nor things to come, hostile powers, height nor depth, nor any other created thing will have the power to separate us from the love of God that is in Christ Jesus our Lord." (Romans 8:35-39)

I've heard women who are enduring hardships question whether God is there for them or not. Of course, the Bible never says that "feeling God's presence" is a sign that He's there with us. It's not about an emotional or physical feeling. It's about knowing God through reading the Bible daily. When you know Who God is, you'll know that He keeps His promises.

When Jesus says that He's with believers until the end of time, we don't question His presence just because we can't "feel" Him or because conditions are painful at the moment. He is there in the storm with you.

Through the inspiration of the Holy Spirit, the apostle Paul wrote the powerful and encouraging Romans chapter 8. In verse 35, he asks the rhetorical question, "Who can separate us from the love of Christ?" The word *separate* used here is transliterated *chōrizō* in Koine Greek. It means to "go away," or "to make room between," with the point being that nothing is powerful enough to put distance between believers and Christ.

This passage names a number of conditions that can't result in believers being apart from Christ's love, including when we're in distress. The word *distress* in Koine Greek, *stenochōria,* means to feel trapped and anguished within the confines of a small space and unable to find a way out of problems. Perhaps you can relate to that feeling. I've sure been there.

Again, this passage points out that when we're distressed and feeling trapped or hopeless, this distress cannot separate us from Christ's love. He won't abandon us when we're facing hardships, because His love for His flock remains constant.

Speaking of Jesus' flock, this passage also compares those who are suffering as "sheep to be slaughtered." What a helpless feeling we endure when our lives feel out-of-control! Yet, once again, we're comforted by God's Word as we're reminded in this passage that we're never alone.

This is followed by reassurance that in all of our hardships *"we are more than conquerors through Him who loved us."* Notice how Paul - who suffered tremendously during his apostleship - words this passage in the second person "we" because he's including himself in this list of challenges that believers endure.

When this passage uses the word conquerors (*hupernikaō* in Koine Greek), it means "extremely victorious." Here's a reassurance of triumphing through or over hardship - not because of our own abilities - because of Christ's love for believers.

This is a promise of more than being able to endure the hardship. This is a promise of triumph and victory! Being victorious may look

CHAPTER 15: MORE THAN CONQUERORS

different than your exceptions, but it will be meaningful and filled with growth because that's how God leads us.

So, distress and other conditions can't separate us from Christ's love. And the passage continues with further lists - death, life, angels, rulers, uncertainties, hostile powers, heights, depths, other created things - to show that *nothing* can separate you from God's love.

In other words, there's no circumstance, person, or power which could take you away from the love of God within Christ Jesus. Even if you feel abandoned, alone, or like your prayers aren't being heard: if you're a believer who has put your trust into Jesus as your Lord and Savior and you believe the Gospel, then you can trust that His love for you is unbreakable. You are loved, dear sister!

Reflection Questions:

1. Does that make sense that God's presence isn't measured by whether we can "feel" Him or not? How does daily Bible study help with knowing and trusting God's attributes and promises?
2. Have you ever worried whether God loved you? Does this passage help to reassure you that you're loved?
3. What are some ways to keep your focus upon God's love, instead of upon needless worries?
4. Do your times of suffering draw you closer to God? In what ways?

Chaper 16: God of all Comfort

"Blessed be the God and Father of our Lord Jesus Christ, the Father of mercies and the God of all comfort, who comforts us in all our affliction, so that we may be able to comfort those who are in any kind of affliction, through the comfort we ourselves receive from God. (2 Corinthians 1:3-4).

Isn't this passage comforting? Our Creator is the God of all comfort and He comforts us during our afflictions. That way, we're able to comfort others who are going through an affliction because of the comfort we receive from God. This passage is like a group hug! God comforts you, and through receiving His comfort, you're able to comfort others who are in similar struggles.

Sometimes women tell me that they fear they don't "deserve" God's love or forgiveness. Yet, passages like this one are reminders that God's love extends to others through you. Besides that, God's love is from His grace and mercy. The more that we study the Bible, the more familiar we become with God's attributes so that we trust His promises.

This passage begins with praising God: *Blessed be the God*, with the Koine Greek word for blessed *eulogetos*, meaning *adorable*. We should always adore, praise and worship God, through the sunshine and the storms of life. Praising God is a natural outgrowth of trusting God. Our

CHAPTER 16: GOD OF ALL COMFORT

purpose is to glorify God in all that we do.

The passage refers to God as "the Father of mercies," which emphasizes God's abundantly merciful character. We especially see God's mercy in Jesus' life, death, and resurrection for us while we were rebellious sinners. Salvation is a gift of God's mercy and grace.

Next, the passage says that our Creator is "the God of all comfort." In the original New Testament Biblical language of Koine Greek, the word *comfort* is transliterated as *paraklesis*, which means consolation or encouragement. This refers to God's compassionate nature in consoling us during our hardships.

He may allow the suffering to continue, yet it's important to understand that God actively comforts us when we're suffering. As the passage says, God comforts us *in* all our affliction, not *from* our affliction. Comforting you doesn't mean that God instantly fixes situations. It means that in the midst of an uncomfortable situation, God helps you to stay encouraged and peaceful. It's like being in the eye of a hurricane.

There's always a reason why God allows suffering, even if we don't understand it at the time. This is why the Bible exhorts us to trust in the Lord with all of our heart.

This passage hints at one reason why God may have allowed you to suffer: so that you could comfort others enduring similar ordeals. God comforts you in your hardship, so that you can pass His comfort along to others who are suffering.

So, God's presence during our suffering doesn't necessarily mean that He stops the pain. Sometimes He miraculously heals and fixes situations, according to His will and timing. But if He allows the painful situation to continue, we can trust that He's actively present with us in our suffering. God sees your hardship and offers His compassion and comfort to help you to endure and grow.

It's helpful to remember prior hardships that God allowed you to endure. What blessings or lessons may have come out of those hardships? Examples might include drawing closer to God, becoming stronger, having increased compassion for those who similarly suffer, gaining a stronger desire to volunteer, having a heart for the lost, and so forth.

Turn to God in the midst of your struggles, dear sister. Read His Word and pray for His comfort, strength, and wisdom. Trust that God has a purpose for everything, including painful circumstances. If you need help trusting Him, pray for your trust to be increased. Remember that God is growing you in ways that will help others.

Reflection Questions:

1. What are some helpful ways that you can comfort a friend who's enduring a struggle that you've previously endured?
2. In what ways has the Father of mercies been merciful to you?
3. Does that make sense that God can comfort you while you're going through an uncomfortable situation? Has that happened to you, and what was it like?
4. How has your trust in the Lord increased? Does this help you when you're facing hardships?

Chapter 17: Jesus, the Suffering Servant

"He is despised and rejected of men; a man of sorrows, and acquainted with grief: and we hid as it were our faces from him; he was despised, and we esteemed him not. Surely he hath borne our griefs, and carried our sorrows: yet we did esteem him stricken, smitten of God, and afflicted. But he was wounded for our transgressions, he was bruised for our iniquities: the chastisement of our peace was upon him; and with his stripes we are healed. All we like sheep have gone astray; we have turned every one to his own way; and the Lord hath laid on him the iniquity of us all." (Isaiah 53:3-6)

Isaiah's prophetic description of the Messiah Jesus Christ as "The Suffering Servant" shows that His death on the cross was part of God's plan of redemption that He revealed after the fall:

"And I will put enmity between you and the woman, and between your seed and her seed; He shall bruise your head, and you shall bruise his heel." (Genesis 3:15)

Both of these passages speak about our sinless Lord and Savior Jesus' willingness to suffer and die on the cross, to defeat the devil and sin.

Jesus sympathizes with your suffering because He loves you and because He endured horrendous suffering during His earthly ministry. Jesus was rejected, persecuted, slandered, flogged, and crucified. He understands what believers are enduring, because He went through suffering Himself as Hebrews 4:15 summarizes:

> *"For we do not have a High Priest who cannot sympathize with our weaknesses, but was in all points tempted as we are, yet without sin."*

The passage at the top of this chapter from Isaiah 53:4-6 describes Jesus' substitutionary suffering on our behalf. He was sinless, yet He was crucified and pierced for our sins. Jesus bore the wrath that we all deserve (Romans 3:23), so that our sins could be forgiven the moment that we put our faith in Jesus as our Lord and Savior.

Just as Jesus suffered for a reason, so too do we suffer for a reason. Be assured that your suffering has meaning and purpose, dear sister. In Jesus' life, death, and resurrection, there's victory over sin and death.

In your moments of hardship, look to the cross. Pray for God to strengthen you. We may not realize until much later what the purpose was for our suffering, yet we can trust that God does.

Reflection Questions:

1. Does it reassure you to know that Jesus empathizes with your pain, because He endured suffering on earth?
2. How does knowing that God's plan of redemption goes back to Genesis 3:15 (and even before), help you to trust God's sovereign plan for your life?
3. How has the way that you deal with hardships changed since you put your trust in Jesus and became a Christian?

CHAPTER 17: JESUS, THE SUFFERING SERVANT

4. Have you ever been falsely taught that God always heals everyone who asks "in the right way"? What are your thoughts about that false teaching now?

Chapter 18: We Do Not Lose Heart

"Therefore we do not lose heart. Though outwardly we are wasting away, yet inwardly we are being renewed day by day." (2 Corinthians 4:16)

The phrase, "we do not lose heart" is a powerful summary of the strength and endurance that God gives to us during trials. Life is a constant juggling act for a lot of us women, who care for our husband, children, elderly parents, in addition to other responsibilities and challenges. It's easy to feel overwhelmed to the point of just wanting to run away and hide.

This verse is a call to persevere. Of course, we shouldn't try to endure with our own strength, but with the strength that Christ gives us in response to our prayers. We keep going because of the eternal hope that Christ has given to us. The strength to "not lose heart" comes through Christ.

The second part of this verse contrasts that we are all physically aging and "outwardly we are wasting away." That's not a pleasant thought, but it's the reality for this world. Praise God that believers can instead fix our eyes upon Jesus and trust that "inwardly we are being renewed day by day." This is an inward spiritual renewal, in contrast to physical outward aging, illness, or injury.

CHAPTER 18: WE DO NOT LOSE HEART

This isn't like Gnosticism or Christian Science which insist that the material world is an illusion and only the spiritual world is real. God is the Creator of our physical bodies. He knitted us together in our mother's womb. Everything that God creates is good. And yet, ever since the fall recorded in Genesis 3, humanity is subject to physical death. And while our earthly body ages and decays, inwardly the Holy Spirit helps believers to be sanctified and grow more Christlike. We also look forward to our glorified bodies that will be free of all sin, sickness and death for eternity (1 Corinthians 15:42-44; Philippians 3:20-21; 1 John 3:2).

Changes occurring to our physical bodies and our inward beings can both present us with challenges. While the inward renewal is definitely a positive light for believers, the sanctification process can be challenging. Sanctification means being "set apart," so it can be painful as it demands humility, self-denial (Luke 9:23) and spiritual warfare (Ephesians 6:10-18) as we battle against the evil one's harassment and temptations.

While our physical suffering is real, our sanctification and inner renewal is also an encouragement. God gives strength and comfort for enduring both outward and inward struggles.

So when this verse says "outwardly we are wasting away," it's an encouraging reminder that this world is our temporary home. Our physical bodies are temporary. Our true home is in eternity with Christ and other believers in our glorified bodies. You are not alone in your struggles, sweet sister! Every true believer in Jesus undergoes similar growing pains of sanctification and faces hardships. You're also not alone because Jesus has promised to be with us always. May you continue to keep Him front and center in your focus and in your prayers.

Reflection Questions:

1. In what ways are you growing and being renewed through the sanctification process?
2. Does it encourage you to consider that your physical struggles are offset by your inner renewal?
3. What habits (like daily Bible reading, praying frequently, etc.) help you to stay focused upon Jesus?
4. How do you persevere during trials so that you don't lose heart, as 2 Corinthians 4:16 emphasizes?

Chapter 19: God is the Strength of Your Heart

"Whom have I in heaven but you? And there is nothing on earth that I desire besides you. My flesh and my heart may fail, but God is the strength of my heart and my portion forever." (Psalm 73:25-26)

Sometimes we struggle with jealousy at another person's success, even when we know that covetousness is forbidden. It just doesn't seem fair that people who behave in unethical or even wicked ways are allowed to prosper, when we work hard to live by biblical principles and yet we aren't acknowledged. Even Job observed this apparent disparity (Job 21).

As usual, God has included every human condition in the Bible. Although people may have different customs compared to Biblical times, inwardly people still struggle with the same relationship issues. That includes being frustrated when the wicked prosper, while righteous people seem to suffer.

God addresses this exact situation in Psalm 73, where He teaches us about the futility of envy and jealousy and how we can trust God even when life seems unfair. Envy is wanting what someone else has, and jealousy is fearing the loss of what you have. The Bible does talk about

God's jealousy in a positive way, as He's protecting us from idolatry (c.f., Exodus 34:14). Human jealousy, in contrast, is usually a work of the flesh (Galatians 5:20).

Psalm 73 is a beautiful example of Asaph, the chief musician, pouring out his heart to God, including wrestling with feelings that we may be embarrassed to share with God. Remember that God knows the secrets of our heart, and calls for us to model after the Psalms with being authentic and transparent with God, as Psalm 44:21 says:

> *"Would not God have discovered it, since he knows the secrets of the heart?"*

Psalm 73 describes that Asaph almost stumbled and slipped spiritually speaking, because he was envious of the prosperity of the wicked. He described the wicked as being well-fed and shielded from consequences for their actions. They were also prideful and violent, and they spoke with malice and threatened oppression. The Psalmist said:

> *"Behold, these are the wicked; always at ease, they increase in riches. All in vain have I kept my heart clean and washed my hands in innocence."*

The Psalmist's frustration at the apparent unfairness, was where he almost stumbled and slipped spiritually. He had forgotten to trust in God. While God doesn't promise "fairness" as we think about it in a human way, God knows and provides for our needs.

We also learn in Psalm 73 that God allows the wicked to prosper as part of His judgment for their wicked ways. They might temporarily enjoy their earth life, but unless they repent and trust in the Messiah Jesus Christ, they're heading to an eternity of torment.

This is similar to the warnings in Romans 1:28:

CHAPTER 19: GOD IS THE STRENGTH OF YOUR HEART

"And since they did not see fit to acknowledge God, God gave them up to a debased mind to do what ought not to be done."

We see this in Scripture where God has patience with unrepentant sinners . . . to a point. Then, He exercises His judgment. Sometimes that involves God allowing the sinners to sin without restraint (c.f., Judges 9:23; Samuel 16:14). We also know from Proverbs 11:2 and 16:18 that pridefulness leads to destruction. Psalm 73 says that God sets the wicked in slippery places and makes them fall to ruin.

The point is that we shouldn't allow ourselves to sin by being jealous or envious of the wicked prospering. Another point is that only God knows if someone is saved or not, so we should avoid assuming that a person will go to hell for their punishment. God is patient with sinners (Romans 2:4; 2 Peter 3:9), although persistent unrepentant sin leads to consequences (Genesis 6:3; Proverbs 29:1), and rejecting the Gospel leads to eternal damnation (Matthew 25:41,46; John 3:35; 2 Thessalonians 1:8-9).

Once Asaph realized that God isn't unfair by allowing the wicked to prosper, he expressed his relief and repented for his previous jealousy:

> *"When my soul was embittered, which I was pricked in heart, I was brutish and ignorant; I was like a beast toward you. Nevertheless, I am continually with you; you hold my right hand. You guide me with your counsel, and afterward you will receive me to glory."*
> *(Psalm 73:21-23)*

Repentance is essential to restoring our relationship with God (c.f., Isaiah 55:7; Acts 3:19; 1 John 1:9), as the Psalmist's example shows us in Psalm 73. After repenting, he praises God with the verses which this chapter opens with:

> *"Whom have I in heaven but you? And there is nothing on earth that I desire besides you. My flesh and my heart may fail, but God is the strength of my heart and my portion forever."* (Psalm 73: 25-26)

What a beautiful heartfelt example of a repentant heart filled with gratitude toward God! This Psalm is a perfect example of how our tangled mess of jealousy and envy can cause us to sin and disrupt our trust in the Lord. Envy is also unhealthy, as Proverbs 14:30 instructs:

> *"A tranquil heart gives life to the flesh, but envy makes the bones rot."*

At a time when we need God the most, jealousy and envy are like retreating into isolation instead of drawing near to God. Nonetheless, everyone experiences envy and jealousy at times. The key is to catch yourself engaging in these feelings, and then repentantly bringing them to God for His forgiveness. By praying for God's help and telling him about all of your uncomfortable feelings, God can give you wisdom to help you to stop envying the wicked's apparent prosperity. God helps us through this process when we turn to Him.

Reflection Questions:

1. Can you recall a time when you were envious of someone's success that you felt like they didn't earn or deserve? What did you learn from the experience? Did you repent for your envy and draw closer to God as a result?
2. What are ways to stay reminded that God is sovereign, and is in charge of everyone and everything? Does this comfort you to realize that God's in control?

CHAPTER 19: GOD IS THE STRENGTH OF YOUR HEART

3. Do you share the Psalmist's feelings that it's a relief to know that God allows the wicked to prosper as part of His judgment toward them?
4. Does the Bible ever tell us that God is always fair, in the way that we define fairness? What attributes instead would you use to describe the way that God deals with wickedness?

Chapter 20: Rejoicing Together

"If one member suffers, all suffer together; if one member is honored, all rejoice together." (1 Corinthians 12:26)

When you're struggling through a trial, do you tend to isolate or do you reach out to other Christians for prayer and encouragement? It's tempting to isolate, as you may feel embarrassed about your situation or perhaps you fear you'd burden others with your prayer requests.

1 Corinthians 12:26 is one of many passages that emphasizes the importance of fellowship and coming together with other believers in times of sorrow. This verse is part of a discourse about the body of believers being compared to a human body, with each part of the body being equally important. Believers are collectively referred to as *the body of Christ* in 1 Corinthians 12:27. Christ is the head of the body (Colossians 1:18; Ephesians 1:22-23).

Romans 12:4-5 says that this one body of believers has many members. Each member has different functions, just as different parts of our human body have different functions. As Christians, we are all united with Christ and with one another, functioning collectively as His hands and feet in the world to fulfill The Great Commission. Each member of the body has an equally important role.

CHAPTER 20: REJOICING TOGETHER

The Bible teaches that Christians shouldn't isolate, but instead we should bear each others' burdens and pray for one another. When 1 Corinthians 12:26 says that if one part suffers, every part suffers, this is a call for unity during times of struggle. When one part of the body of believers suffers or conversely when one member is rejoicing, it affects the entire body of Christ.

Fellowship means spending time with other believers and developing a bond of authentic sharing and caring. Romans 12:15 tells us to "Rejoice with those who rejoice; mourn with those who mourn" and Galatians 6:2 instructs us to "Carry each other's burdens, and in this way you will fulfill the law of Christ." This is of course a fulfillment of the commandment to love our neighbor as ourselves.

Perhaps you're better at carrying others' burdens, than you are in sharing about your needs and struggles. You may be shy about revealing personal details, and sister it is wise to be cautious around those who are prone to gossip. Yet, that's different than asking for prayer requests. We deepen our relationships with our sisters in Christ by sharing our burdens with them. You don't need to go into the details with your situation if there's concerns about gossip; however, it's important to share enough and ask for prayer and encouragement during your trials.

Fellowship is much more than sharing church potlucks together. It's about sharing our burdens with one another and lifting each other up in prayer. It's about sharing encouraging and applicable Bible verses with each other. It's about rejoicing in the triumphs and crying together during the turbulence.

If you're shy or have social anxiety, you can pray for God to help you with courage to overcome shyness. On a practical level, this means attending a biblically solid local church and staying after the service. It means saying *Hi* to people at church and having conversations where you ask how they and their family are doing, and look for common interests such as homeschooling or gardening. The Bible exhorts us to spend time together, specifically at the local church as we see in Hebrews 10:24-25:

> *"And let us consider how we may spur one another on toward love and good deeds, not giving up meeting together, as some are in the habit of doing, but encouraging one another - and all the more as you see the Day approaching."*

The Day in this passage refers to the Day of the Lord: Jesus' second coming and Judgment Day when the sheep and the goats will be sorted (Matthew 25:31-32). As the Day of the Lord approaches, it's even more important for believers to gather and encourage one another.

Reflection Questions:

1. How do you feel about sharing your struggles with a sister in Christ, and asking her for prayer?
2. Do you belong to a local church? If not, why not? And if yes, do you spend time after the service talking with other members?
3. If you're concerned about burdening your friends or being gossiped about by over-sharing about your problems, what are some ways you can reign in your sharing while still being authentic and asking for prayers?
4. What are some fun ways to gather with your sisters in Christ, in addition to church events? Which of these gatherings can you initiate and host?

Chapter 21: Joyful in Hope

"Be joyful in hope, patient in affliction, faithful in prayer." (Romans 12:12)

What an encouraging verse and reminder to stay hopeful, be patient and to pray! Under the inspiration of the Holy Spirit, the apostle Paul wrote these words as part of a passage about how to live a Christ-centered life, especially in the midst of trials. The original Biblical language in these words also gives depth to their meaning. Let's look at the three parts of this verse, and how to apply them to your life:

Be joyful in hope

The word *joyful* is often translated as *rejoicing* in other Bible translations. In the original Koine Greek language joyful/rejoicing is *chairō* meaning to be full of cheer. This refers to a deep, abiding joy based upon your hope in Christ and your assurance of God's promises. It's the joy that is the fruit of the Spirit (Galatians 5:22), and not a fleeting circumstantial type of joy.

This verse reminds us to not base our joy upon our circumstances, which will shift and change. Sometimes we might think, "Well, I'll be happy once my life improves." But our joy isn't dependent upon circumstances. Instead, our joy is from our salvation and our eternal relationship with God. This world is challenging for all Christians. You're not alone in your trials, as Jesus promised that in this world we Christians would face troubles (John 16:33).

Patient in affliction

The word *patient* here in Koine Greek transliteration is *hupomenō*, which refers to perseverance while enduring trials. It's a present-tense active word, so it means to be patient, steadfast, and persevering *right now*.

Of course, we must pray for God to give us the strength to persevere and be patient. We can't do this on our own strength, especially when we're suffering.

Faithful in prayer

Faithful is *proskartereō* in Koine Greek transliteration. This means "to be earnest," "to continually wait on," or "to persevere" in present and active tense. So this is calling us to be persistent in prayer right now.

Persistent prayer is different than the repetitious prayer that Jesus warned about in Matthew 6:7. That type of prayer was a mindless mechanical or a theatrical repetitious prayer, similar to pagan chants.

The exhortation to be devoted to, or faithful in, persistent prayers refers to heartfelt sincere prayers. These prayers aren't formulas that you read from a recipe book, but are prayers of sincerely worshiping God, sharing your thoughts and feelings, and asking Him for help for yourself or others.

CHAPTER 21: JOYFUL IN HOPE

We are called to pray without ceasing in 1 Thessalonians 5:16-18).

Reflection Questions:
1. What comes to mind when you think of the term *devoted*? What does it mean to you, to be devoted to prayer?
2. What are some ways to remind yourself to pray more often?
3. When someone asks you to pray for them, do you stop and pray at that moment? Or do you keep a prayer journal to help you to remember to pray on their behalf?
4. How does reviewing what you're grateful to God for, help you to stay joyful?

Chapter 22: Rest in Christ

"Come to me, all of you who are weary and burdened, and I will give you rest." (Matthew 11:28)

In addition to any trials you're enduring, you have daily responsibilities to manage. At times, this can feel overwhelming, especially if there's no one to sufficiently help you (or if you're shy about delegating). Constant worry, health concerns, family needs, insufficient sleep and lack of exercise or proper nutrition can all lead you to feel drained.

Yet, God didn't build us like a machine that can keep going nonstop. You need rest, dear sister! If you're feeling weary and burdened, please remember our Lord and Savior Jesus' invitation to come to Him. Set down your burdens at the foot of the cross, and tell Him about all of your concerns.

If you're a do-it-yourself gal, you may have difficulty at first in realizing that we can't do anything in our own strength. It can be a tough habit to break, to realize that you don't need to do everything by yourself. Some of us were raised to believe that asking for help is a sign of weakness! If that sounds like you, let's dive into encouragement from Scripture:

Philippians 4:13 says, *"I can do all things through Christ who strengthens me."* This verse which the apostle Paul wrote while he was in prison, reminds us that our strength comes from God and not from ourselves.

In John 15:5, Jesus teaches us that without Him we can't bear fruit: *"I am the vine, you are the branches. He who abides in Me, and I in him, bears much fruit; for without Me you can do nothing."*

Psalm 127:1 offers a convicting reminder that anything we try to do without God is futile, and the results of our efforts probably won't last: *"Unless the Lord builds the house, the builders labor in vain. Unless the Lord watches over the city, the guards stand watch in vain."*

Isaiah 40:29-31 teaches that God provides strength to those who trust Him: *"He gives power to the weak, and to those who have no might He increases strength. Even the youths shall utterly fall, but those who wait on the Lord shall renew their strength; they shall mount up with wings like eagles, they shall run and not be weary, they shall walk and not faint."*

Psalm 46:1 reminds us that God is there for us: *"God is our refuge and strength, an ever-present help in trouble."*

Ephesians 6:10 confirms that our strength comes from God's power, not from ourselves: *"Finally, be strong in the Lord and in His mighty power."*

Colossians 1:11 summarizes that God is the source of all power and strength: *"Being strengthened with all power according to His glorious might so that you may have great endurance and patience."*

Hebrews 13:6 encourages us to not be afraid because God is there with us: *"So we say with confidence, 'The Lord is my helper; I will not be afraid. What can mere mortals do to me?'"*

Trying to power through our day in our own strength leads to exhaustion and frustration! In addition to the strength factor, there's also the question of whose will is leading you? Your own will, or God's will? There are so many reasons to turn to God as our source for everything that we need. May our do-it-yourself approach to life be retired for good!

Reflection Questions:

1. What or who influenced you in the past to take a do-it-yourself approach to life? What are your thoughts about this approach now?
2. Can you think of a time when you reached out in prayer to God, asking for Him to give you strength? What changes did you notice when you turned to God instead of trying to use your own strength?
3. How do you react when others offer to help you? Do you welcome being helped, or do you tend to push it away with an excuse?
4. When you're tired, are you able to take a nap without guilt? Why or why not?

Chapter 23: Don't Worry, Pray Instead

"Do not be anxious about anything, but in every situation, by prayer and petition, with thanksgiving, present your requests to God. And the peace of God, which transcends all understanding, will guard your hearts and minds in Christ Jesus." (Philippians 4:6-7)

It seems like there's so much to be anxious about in the world, doesn't it? One glance at social media, and you're chewing your fingernails from the posts about how awful everything is becoming. You worry about the future, your family, finances, health, and safety.

Worry means the thoughts we have about specific scenarios and particular concerns. *Anxiety* is the physical and emotional reactions to worry. Someone can feel anxious in general without knowing what they're specifically worried about.

Yet, God doesn't want us to be anxious or to worry. In fact, He commands us to *not* be worried or anxious, but instead to turn to Him in prayer. It's a command to trust Him.

Sometimes, it may feel challenging to trust God during hardships, especially if you've been praying and nothing has seemed to change. The first of the month is creeping up and your checkbook balance is still too low to pay the rent. Your son's teacher is calling you in for meetings. Your husband is spending more time at work than at home. You cry out to God, yet things seem to get worse.

God says in the midst of all of this: "Do not be anxious about anything." He didn't say to be anxious about some things, but not others. He said to not be anxious about *anything*.

When we closely examine our worry or anxiety responses, they're rooted in believing that we're in control. There's this sense that if we can anticipate upcoming troubles, then we can avoid them. Now, this is not to say that we should act irresponsibly. We do need to work, plan, budget, and save. We just need to do all of that while trusting God, instead of being anxious or worrying.

In Philippians 4:6-7, we're exhorted to make our petitions known to God with thanksgiving. This means praying about everything that's concerning us, and asking for God's help with thankfulness that He's our loving Creator Who has helped us many times. God will meet the needs of believers, often in unexpected ways (which is why we don't hand God a to-do list or a script that we want Him to follow). We share our needs and requests with Him in prayer, while trusting Him to help us according to His will and His timing.

One of my favorite parts of this passage is about the peace which surpasses understanding. When we turn to God with faith, trust, and thanksgiving, He transforms us! He may not fix what's going on around us, but He will give us peaceful hearts and minds to endure our trials. This is a true peace that makes no logical sense from a human perspective. From a biblical worldview, we're grateful that God replaces our anxious feelings and worrisome thoughts with His supernatural peace.

In this passage, we're told that God's peace will guard our hearts and minds in Christ Jesus. How lovely that God's peace anchors us to His truth, and keeps our focus upon the Gospel. We approach our responsibilities with grace and joy, instead of with anxiety or worry.

CHAPTER 23: DON'T WORRY, PRAY INSTEAD

Jesus comforts us with His words of reassurance, as He teaches in the Sermon on the Mount about the futility of worry:

- "Therefore I tell you, do not worry about your life, what you will eat or drink; or about your body, what you will wear. Is not life more than food, and the body more than clothes?" (Matthew 6:25)
- "Look at the birds of the air; they do not sow or reap or store away in barns, and yet your heavenly Father feeds them. Are you not much more valuable than they? (Matthew 6:26)
- "Can any one of you by worrying add a single hour to your life?" (Matthew 6:27)

May these words of our Lord and Savior rest deeply in your heart and mind, dear sister, and bring you peace and comfort.

Reflection Questions:

1. Have you ever used unhealthful behaviors to try to calm your worries or anxiety? What were the results?
2. What are some ways that you can notice when you're anxious or worried, so that you can stop and pray?
3. Jesus emphasized that worrying doesn't help anything. In what ways have you noticed that worry hasn't helped you, but perhaps instead harms you?
4. Do you have an area in your home with a Bible, reading lamp, and chair where you can go for study, prayer, and reflection?

Chapter 24: Hope in Eternal Glory

"For I consider that the sufferings of this present time are not worth comparing with the glory that is to be revealed to us." (Romans 8:18)

While our suffering is real, it's temporary in the scope of eternity. The pain you're enduring is a hard-won battle in your walk with Christ, helping you to grow more like Him. God is using your struggles to help you to draw closer to Him and to learn important lessons in spiritual growth.

Romans 8:18 acknowledges the reality of suffering, as part of our Christian life. As we suffer, we identify with Christ (c.f., 1 Peter 4:13). "As we share abundantly in Christ's sufferings, so through Christ we share abundantly in comfort too" (2 Corinthians 1:5).

The Bible doesn't deny the reality of suffering. In fact, the Bible says that all Christians can expect trouble, including persecution and spiritual warfare (John 16:33; 2 Timothy 3:12). Jesus also said we Christians are blessed when we are reviled and persecuted for His name (Matthew 5:11-12). The apostle Peter under the inspiration of the Holy Spirit said:

CHAPTER 24: HOPE IN ETERNAL GLORY

"If you are insulted for the name of Christ, you are blessed, because the Spirit of glory and of God rests upon you." (1 Peter 4:14)

The point is that it's normal for Christians to suffer in this life. Yet, we can't even compare our suffering with the glory that we'll find in eternity (c.f., Romans 8:18). The word *glory* in the original biblical language of Koine Greek is transliterated *doxa*, which means majesty, honor, and praise.

This refers to the spiritual transformation we'll experience in the New Heaven with Jesus. There will be no more pain, sin, or tears. Only perfect peace, joy, and love in the presence of Jesus.

We don't know *when* Jesus will return, or *when* we'll go to the New Heaven. Yet, we do know that it will happen according to God's perfect will and timing. We must trust in the Lord's timing, as God knows the exact time for our departure from earth. Romans 8:18 says that our present suffering is not worthy to be compared to the eternal joy that awaits us. In the meantime, may we hold an eternal view and keep our hope fixed upon Jesus.

Reflection Questions:

1. Are you able to keep an eternal view with hope for your eternity with Christ? What helps you to keep this view?
2. Does thinking about your eternal future help you to withstand the temporary suffering in this world?
3. Do you often think about Jesus' teaching in John 17:14-16 that we are *in* this world, but not *of* this world? How does that knowledge help you to cope?
4. Even though this world is temporary for us, in what ways does God expect us to be a good citizen of this world? Please read Titus 3:1-2 for examples.

Chapter 25: The Indwelling Holy Spirit

"*For God gave us a Spirit not of fear but of power and love and self-control.*" (2 Timothy 1:7)

The apostle Paul experienced great hardship after his conversion to Christianity. He was beaten, stoned, slandered, persecuted, and imprisoned. He wrote the words of our opening verse from prison, where he was facing execution. So, for Paul to tell us under the Holy Spirit's inspiration, to not be afraid is remarkable.

This verse emphasizes the indwelling Holy Spirit (*Pneuma* in Koine Greek) within all Christians. This is the Third Person of the Holy Trinity, residing within everyone who believes the Gospel and has put their faith in Jesus as their Lord and Savior. How remarkable that in the face of hardship, the Holy Spirit is our advocate and encourager!

Not only is the Holy Spirit within believers, but His attributes are within us as well. There is no fear in the Holy Spirit, only power, love and self-control. Let's dive deeper into these attributes:

The Spirit of Power: The Koine Greek word for *power* is transliterated as *dunamis* which stems from the root word dynamis. This refers to God's dynamic and transformative force, strength, ability, and power.

This is reassuring as we face challenges, to rely upon God's power instead of our own resources. God's power is far beyond our own human strength. We see an example of this in Zechariah 4:6, when

CHAPTER 25: THE INDWELLING HOLY SPIRIT

Zerubbabel was feeling overwhelmed trying to rebuild the temple after the exile. Listen to this reassurance for all believers:

"Then He said to me, 'This is the word of the Lord to Zerubbabel saying, 'Not by might nor by power, but by My Spirit,' says the Lord of hosts.'"

Self-help gurus claim that they can help to "empower" us. Yet, we can't do anything without the power of the Holy Spirit within us. Pray for God to help you to stop trying to power through situations, and to instead lean into Him. It's about God's power.

The Spirit of Love: The word *love* in this section is *agapaō* in Koine Greek (usually pronounced *agape* in English), which refers to the highest form of love in the Bible. Agapeō is the sacrificial love expressed in John 3:16 about God so loved the world, and in Jesus' command to love one another in John 13:34-35.

The Bible describes other forms of love such as romantic love (*eros*); brotherly love or friendship love (*philia*); and family love (*storge*). These types of love can overlap with agape (for example you can have *agape* sacrificial love combined with your *storge* family love), yet agape love is described in the Bible as the most selfless form of love.

The Holy Spirit within us gives us the ability to love selflessly and sacrificially.

The Spirit of Self-Control: When Christians discuss the list of the Fruit of the Spirit from Galatians 5:22-23, they usually groan that "self-control" is the fruit that they're working on. Who among us hasn't needed more self-control to resist a second helping of chocolate cake at the church potluck? Or to resist that sale on those cute boots that you don't need because you already own similar pairs?

Self-control is the Koine Greek word transliterated *enkrateia*, derived from the Greek words for *in* and *strength*. This means having wisdom or having a disciplined mind to overcome temptations and impulses. So, the Bible's definition of self-control is for us to be thinkers in situations that tempt us. We are to use our heads instead of our impulsivity.

Boiled down, then, this means to be alert and sober-minded enough to pray for the Holy Spirit to give us self-control. So if you're in a situation that's tempting you to over-spend, over-eat, relapse on an old addiction, contact an ex, over-indulge, or some other behavior that you know is wrong or unhealthful - stop and pray for God to help you to make wise decisions.

2 Timothy 1:7 is a powerful reminder that we're never alone in our struggles. The Holy Spirit resides inside of us, ready to lead and guide us in every part of our lives.

Reflection Questions:

1. Have you prayed for God's help in a situation where you were tempted? What happened?
2. Can you think of a time when you loved sacrificially (agape)? What was that like, and did you realize at the time that this agape love was coming from the Holy Spirit?
3. Is it helpful to know that the Holy Spirit's power is within you as a Christian, so that you don't feel afraid of man or of the world?
4. When you feel overwhelmed by responsibilities, how can you remember to turn to God for His power and strength?

Chapter 26: Wings like Eagles

"But those who hope in the LORD will renew their strength. They will soar on wings like eagles; they will run and not grow weary, they will walk and not faint." Isaiah 40:31

Imagine soaring above your troubles, like an eagle flying high! This encouraging verse from the prophet Isaiah through the Holy Spirit's inspiration promises that those who hope in the Lord will have renewed strength. Let's look deeper at this verse and its practical application to our lives.

Let's first examine the context of this verse. It was part of Isaiah chapter 40, which was written as a comforting encouragement to the Israelites who were suffering in exile during the Babylonian captivity. They'd lost their homes, their nation, and their temple because they'd lost their way with idolatry and other sinful practices. The prophet Jeremiah had spoken on behalf of the Lord that their exile would be for 70 years, and then they would return home (Jeremiah 29:10). It was in this context that Isaiah wrote Isaiah 40:31 so they would keep their hope focused upon God, to keep their strength.

So how do we apply this promise to our own lives?

First, there's the importance of having hope in the Lord. The word *hope* in this verse is often translated as "wait." The Hebrew for this word is transliterated *qavah*, which means "to look for" or "to wait for." So, hope isn't an emotion, but an active waiting for the Lord with expectation that He will act on your behalf according to His will.

This is way beyond "positive thinking," which involves trying to use our human will to make things happen. *Hope in the Lord* means that you completely trust our sovereign God to act according to His will and His timing. It's trusting that the outcome will be according to His will, and trusting that the outcome will be good (even if it's not the outcome you wanted).

Hope in the Lord is the opposite of what some people do: They pray to God as if giving an order to their waiter. They pray that God would hurry and fulfill this order. Yet, God can see the entire picture, while we can only see a fragment. God can also see why all of the elements must first fall into place, so His timing is perfect.

It's a shame that some people get discouraged because their prayers didn't seem to be answered immediately according to their specifications. God isn't a waiter or a genie. God has a much better plan and timing than we could ever dream of! And yes, sometimes prayers are answered in painful ways, but always God uses these circumstances to draw us closer to Him.

So, "hope in the Lord" means patiently waiting for the Lord's perfect timing, trusting in the Lord, and expecting only good results from the Lord (again, even if the results are different than what you want). Instead of putting our hope in ourselves or other people or institutions, our hope is in the Lord.

The second part of Isaiah 40:31 promises that those who hope in the Lord will have their strength renewed. Let's look at this deeper:

Renew in Hebrew is transliterated *chalaph*, meaning to alter or change. It is used as an illustration of a new sprout and to describe when something is replaced with something new. When we hope in the Lord, our weak human strength is replaced with God's strength!

CHAPTER 26: WINGS LIKE EAGLES

Isaiah 40:31 next says that those whose hope is in the Lord and whose strength has been renewed will "soar on wings like eagles." The word soar is often translated as "to mount up" and in Hebrew the word means to ascend or climb upward. If you've seen an eagle's wings outstretched as it flies, you'll understand this symbolism for strength. When we hope in the Lord, He gives us the strength to fly above our problems. This doesn't imply that we ignore our problems, or behave irresponsibly. The false teachings of Gnosticism, new age, and Christian Science advise people to pretend that their problems don't exist as a supposed way of making the problems go away. But this isn't Biblical, nor does it work! Flying above our problems is the freedom of trusting God and His plans, including taking action as His wisdom leads you to do.

This verse also promises that those whose hope is in the Lord will be given perseverance and endurance. They will run and not grow weary, and they will walk and not be faint. When we think of the word faint, we usually picture someone losing consciousness and falling over. But in this verse, *faint* in Hebrew means growing tired or becoming weary. So, those who have hope in the Lord will have endurance and won't grow weary.

In other words, when you trust in the Lord, His strength will help you to stay encouraged and not give up. Remember: if you need help in trusting the Lord, pray for God to help you. Pray for Him to increase your hope, your trust, and your patience in His will and His timing. May you find comfort in God's promises, dear sister.

Reflection Questions:

1. Can you recall a time when you tried to power-through a situation, trying to use your own strength? How did that go?
2. Are there any areas of your life where you struggle to trust God?

Why do you think that is? What steps can you take (such as prayer or Bible study) to increase your trust in the Lord?
3. What do you normally do when you feel overwhelmed? Are there any changes you'd like to make in the ways that you normally deal with feeling overwhelmed?
4. What would your life be like if you could trust God with all of your heart?

Chapter 27: Delegating and Sharing Your Burdens

"Moses' father-in-law replied, "This is not good! You're going to wear yourself out and the people too. This job is too heavy a burden for you to handle all by yourself." Exodus 18:17-18

I love this passage in Exodus, where Moses was confronted by his caring father-in-law Jethro, because Moses was trying to single-handedly tackle all of the responsibilities. Everyone needs a Jethro to confront us about our overwork, don't we? We also need a caring Jethro to show us how to delegate responsibilities to others.

Well, God has supplied us with all that we need to learn how to set down our burdens and learn to share and delegate. Let's start with the Biblical context of this passage:

God appointed Moses to lead the Israelites out of slavery in Egypt and into the Promised Land across the Jordan River. It's estimated that Moses led approximately 600,000 men and up to 3 million total Israelites including women and children. Moses was helped by his brother Aaron and his sister Miriam as they followed God's lead.

Yet, Moses took on the enormous task of acting as the sole judge for the inevitable disputes that arose with millions of people. Moses was definitely qualified to be a judge, yet the processes took much of his time and energy. Recognizing that his son-in-law was weary and burdened by this responsibility, Jethro confronted Moses and said that he needed to delegate the judicial duties to elders.

Can you relate to Moses' situation, where you're trying to do everything yourself? Maybe it feels quicker just to do it yourself, instead of taking time to teach and supervise someone else performing the task. Or perhaps there are trust issues, where you doubt someone else could competently complete the task. Maybe it's a fear of appearing weak if you don't do it all yourself. Or you might decide that people will be angry if you ask them for help, and you don't want to bother them. And sometimes, control issues are involved, where you want to be the one in charge either because you know you'll do a better job, or because you're seeking secondary rewards (i.e., attention, praise, increased pay, etc.). Regardless of why, it's important to question "what's the cost of trying to be everything to everyone"?

Jethro's confrontation of Moses illustrates the importance of delegating and asking others for help. In addition, Jethro counseled Moses to delegate to capable and honest people who feared the Lord and who had ethics about not accepting bribes. So, Jethro taught that delegation requires wisdom - God's wisdom. It's not about handing off tasks to the first person we see. It's about praying for God's wisdom in selecting who we'll ask for help, and then also praying for God to give us the strength and boldness to ask for help.

When we delegate to our children, of course, we don't expect them to instantly be knowledgeable about how to complete tasks. We need to patiently help them to learn how to help us. My mother was a do-everything-myself woman when I was a child. One weekend, I stayed at a girlfriend's house and she had many chores to do around the house. I found that I enjoyed helping her with washing the dishes, sweeping the floor, and so forth. When I got home, I talked with my mother about this experience and asked if I could start doing chores to help her. She

CHAPTER 27: DELEGATING AND SHARING YOUR BURDENS

looked surprised and relieved, and she seemed grateful as she gave me chores to do. I believe that children benefit from helping around the house.

The Hebrew word for *burden* in Exodus 18:18 is often translated as *heavy*. In Hebrew, this word means heavy in a figurative and grievous sense. Jethro recognized the strain upon his son-in-law, so he advised Moses to share the burden with others who could help.

Dear sister, God didn't make us to be like machines performing 24/7. We need to rest. Our Heavenly Father rested on the seventh day, and Jesus invites His followers to rest in him:

> *"Come with me by yourselves to a quiet place and get some rest."*
> (Mark 6:31)

Delegating involves trusting God to help you to choose wisely whom and how you ask for help. This is about trusting in the Lord to provide for you. We sometimes act like the world will fall apart if we don't do everything ourselves, yet God is the One Who sustains all of life. Share your emotional and physical burdens with God first of all, and then secondly with those whom God has brought into your life.

Reflection Questions:

1. What are some of the reasons why you may be reluctant to ask for help with tasks and chores?
2. Have you prayed for God to give you wisdom about whom to ask for help?
3. What are some ways that other people (including your children) would be blessed by helping you with chores?
4. In what ways would your life improve if you had some help with your chores?

Chapter 28: Patiently Waiting on God's Timing

"Be strong, and let your heart take courage, all you who wait for the Lord!" (Psalm 31:24)

When you pray for God's help, how do you deal when the situation remains unchanged? Have you ever prayed for God to save someone's life, and that person died anyway? Or when prayers for provision didn't seem to yield help? How do we deal with disappointment when it seems like God isn't answering our prayers?

The Apostle Paul went through this type of situation. Paul described in 2 Corinthians 12:7-10 his persistent struggle that he called a "thorn in his side." Despite praying for relief, God allowed that struggle to stay in Paul's life. Paul didn't describe exactly what the thorn was beyond that he called it a "messenger of Satan." So, speculations about the nature of this situation would be unbiblical.

Paul's situation of seeming to have unanswered prayers is applicable to those who struggle with these questions of why God seems to answer some prayers and not others. The take-away from Paul's description of his struggle, is that Paul realized that the thorn kept him humble. Paul said in verse 7 under the inspiration of the Holy Spirit: "Therefore I will boast all the more gladly of my weaknesses, so that the power of Christ may rest upon me." Paul's example of trusting in and depending upon God's sovereign will is inspiring to all of us when our prayers don't seem to yield relief.

When God doesn't seem to answer a prayer in the way that you asked, this doesn't necessarily mean that He's ignoring or denying your petitions. This could be a matter of waiting upon God's timing. God's will is always perfect, and He is omniscient so He knows all of the factors and people involved. This means that God may be bringing these factors and people into the optimum timing, so this requires our faith, trust, and patience.

We can think of Hannah as an example of a woman who patiently prayed for God to open her womb so that she could have children (1 Samuel 1). Job is often credited with "the patience of Job" for the way that he withstood Satan's temptations to sin in his response to his tragedies. The apostle James under the Holy Spirit's inspiration said that we should be patient just like the farmers who patiently wait for the right conditions for their crops to grow (James 5:7-8).

Yet, we can also see impatience in the Bible, such as David crying out "How long, O Lord? Will you forget me forever?" in Psalm 13. And King Saul lost his crown as a result of his impatience, when he wouldn't wait for the prophet Saul, and instead performed the sacrificial rites of a priest himself (1 Samuel 13:8-14). Abram and Sarai impatiently used Hagar to produce their son, instead of waiting upon God's timing in fulfilling His promise (Genesis 16:1-4).

Patience is a fruit of the indwelling Holy Spirit within believers. The Holy Spirit transforms and strengthens believers so that we can endure frustrations with a peaceful heart, and He teaches us how to respond to challenges in a Christlike manner. The Holy Spirit also convicts us when we're tempted to sin in response to a trial, and He also encourages us to have faith and trust in God.

Dear sister, waiting on the Lord doesn't mean sitting idle with inaction. We can still take steps to improve the situation while submitting to God's will and timing. For example, if you're involved with a health challenge, it's wise to take healthful actions to care for your body while you wait for God to answer your prayers. Of course, we would never take sinful actions that contradict God's commandments. The point is that we shouldn't just sit on the sofa awaiting God's miracle. We need to trust Him while we continue taking responsible actions.

Let's remember the encouraging wisdom of Romans 12:12:

"Rejoice in hope, be patient in tribulation, be constant in prayer."

In the middle of a storm, we call out to God and praise His name. We take shelter and wait for the storm to pass. Then we pray for God to give us the strength for the rebuilding process after the storm. God may not fix the situation or stop the storm, yet He's with us during the storm to supernaturally give us strength, hope, and patience.

Reflection Questions:

1. Can you recall a time when God answered your prayer differently than you expected? What were the blessings from the way that God answered your prayer?
2. When you think about times when God seemed to not answer your prayer (such as for a specific relationship, house, job, etc.) can you see in hindsight how He gave you something better? Can you see evidence that He was protecting you by not giving you the specific situation you'd prayed for?
3. What are your thoughts about God's timing being perfect?
4. How has the Holy Spirit transformed your ability to be patient?

Chapter 29: Take Up Your Cross

"Then Jesus told His disciples, 'If anyone would come after Me, let him deny himself and take up his cross and follow Me.'" (Matthew 16:24)

What does it mean to take up our cross, and is this related to the suffering we're enduring? Jesus' words in Matthew 16:24 follow His conversation with His disciples, particularly with Peter. Jesus had asked His disciples, "Who do people say the Son of Man is?" and Peter confessed, "You are the Christ, the Son of the living God" (Matthew 16:16).

After Peter's confession of Jesus' deity, our Lord began revealing the suffering that He and His followers would endure. First, Jesus proclaimed that He would suffer and die (Matthew 16:21), which Peter objected to. This is when Jesus rebuked Peter and said, "Get behind Me, Satan!" (Matthew 16:23).

This is the context of Jesus proclaiming that His followers would need to take up their cross (Matthew 16:24). Jesus was warning that following Him wouldn't be a sugar-coated path of comfort and prosperity (as some false teachers claim). Instead, followers of Jesus face a life of sacrifice, rejection, self-denial, and a willingness to suffer as He did.

Let's dive deeper into what Jesus said in Matthew 16:24:

- **"If anyone would come after Me"** This is Jesus' open invitation to *anyone* who would follow Him. To come after Jesus means to make a wholehearted commitment to Jesus as your Lord and Savior. He must be Lord over every area of your life. That means obedience to His commandments as He said in John 14, *"If you love me, you will keep my commandments."* This isn't legalism, as it's not about good works for salvation. We are saved by God's grace and mercy through our faith in Jesus, not by our works. However, once we are saved we desire to please God and be obedient.
- **"Let him deny himself"** When temptations arise, Christians are called to deny their human fleshly desires. Self-denial also means to be humble and not prideful. Our overarching desire needs to be for God: to draw closer to Him, to know Him, to study His Word, to trust Him, to love Him, and to obey Him.
- **"And take up his cross"** Jesus clarified the high price that His followers must pay through our willingness to suffer, endure hardships, and even face death for His sake. As Christians, we face certain trials such as rejection for our faith. The cross is also a symbol that we must die to ourselves, meaning that we must put aside our desire for worldly pleasures. When we're in Christ, we're a new creation. Our "old self" from before salvation is gone, and our new self is here (c.f., 2 Corinthians 5:17). Instead of comparing ourselves to other women, we compare ourselves to Christ so that we can reflect His character. In Luke 9:23, Jesus is recorded as saying that we are to take up our cross *daily*.
- **"And follow Me."** This command is a culmination of the previous steps involved with being a Christian. We are literally Christ-followers. This means devoting time daily to study the Bible, to pray, and to serve Him through sharing the Gospel, being an active member of a biblically solid local church, and seeking ways to glorify God.

CHAPTER 29: TAKE UP YOUR CROSS

It's not easy to be a Christian in this fallen world, yet once we are born-again there's no turning back. Jesus taught us through the God-breathed Bible that we as Christians are to enter eternal life with Him through the narrow gate. Jesus warned: "For wide is the gate and broad is the road that leads to destruction, and many enter through it. But small is the gate and narrow the road that leads to life, and only a few find it" (Matthew 7:13-14).

Dear sister, may Jesus' words bring you comfort as you travel the difficult yet necessary narrow road.

Reflection Questions:

1. What are some areas in your life where it's challenging to deny yourself? Have you prayed for God to help you to surrender those areas to Him?
2. In what ways have you faced rejection or slander because of your Christian faith? How did you deal with that, and would you handle it differently now?
3. Are there any temptations you're currently facing? How are you dealing with denying your fleshly desires?
4. What does obedience to Jesus mean to you? Are there any habits or parts of your life that you need to surrender to Him?

Chapter 30: Comfort in Christ

"In Him was life, and that life was the light of all mankind." (John 1:4)

None of the joys or the sorrows that we experience in this world compare to the profound gift of salvation which Jesus gave to us through His shed blood upon the cross. No matter what happens to our bodies in this world, all that matters is that our souls are saved. Thank you, Jesus! I would rather suffer as a Christian in this life, than suffer as a pagan eternally in the next life.

The Biblical study of Jesus is called "Christology," and it involves studying the passages in the Bible that describe and identify Jesus' divine nature. These passages show that Jesus is God and the Creator, with the other two Persons of the Holy Trinity: the Father and the Holy Spirit. Jesus is not a created human. He has always existed.

We can read about Jesus' divinity and how He is co-equal and co-eternal with the Father and the Holy Spirit in John 1 and Colossians 1. So, let's dive in together and read these comforting and encouraging descriptions:

"In the beginning was the Word, and the Word was with God, and the Word was God." (John 1:1)

CHAPTER 30: COMFORT IN CHRIST

The term *Word* is *Logos* in Koine Greek, and refers to Jesus Christ's eternal nature. Logos means the revelation and embodiment of God. The mystery of the Holy Trinity is that Jesus is separate from the Father, yet He and the Holy Spirit are all One God. Our human mind can't really wrap our heads around this easily, and there are no earthly metaphors to describe it without veering into heresy. As an example, trying to compare the Holy Trinity to H20, steam, and ice is the heresy of modalism because it falsely teaches that the Holy Trinity is one person with three different modes.

During times of suffering, it's comforting to realize that Jesus, the eternal Word, isn't distant or detached from our situation. He is God, and He has existed since the beginning. He was and still is intimately involved in Creation as John 1:3 reveals:

> *"Through him all things were made; without him nothing was made that has been made."*

We see a similar teaching of Jesus' involvement in creation in Colossians 1:16-17:

> *"For in him all things were created: things in heaven and on earth, visible and invisible, whether thrones or powers or rulers or authorities; all things have been created through him and for him. He is before all things and in him all things hold together."*

The Bible clearly teaches that God the Father initiated creation (Genesis 1:1) and that He created through or by Jesus (John 1:1-3; Colossians 1:16) with the help of the Holy Spirit (Genesis 1:2; Psalm 104:30). All three Persons of the Holy Trinity are God and our Creator.

When we're suffering, we need to cling to Jesus and be comforted by knowing that Jesus is your Creator and the One who sustains life.

Perhaps, like me, you were previously falsely taught that Jesus was a mortal man who learned how to miraculously heal. Well, Jesus did and still does miraculously heal - because He's God!

Colossians 1:18 offers more encouragement by emphasizing that Jesus is the head of the church body (which includes you if you're a Christian). Jesus leads and has authority over all believers. We are united to Him, and as our leader, Jesus guides us. Just as Jesus promised, you are never alone. He cares about you and every member of His church body.

Jesus was willing to die for our sins out of the deepest love, grace, and mercy. Prior to Jesus' crucifixion, humanity had no hope of having their sins forgiven. Their relationship with God was shattered because of sin. Colossians 1:19-20 summarizes how Jesus saved us sinners from eternal torment:

> *"For God was pleased to have all his fullness dwell in him, and through him to reconcile to himself all things, whether things on earth or things in heaven, by making peace through his blood, shed on the cross."*

Dear sister, I am not trying to minimize any trial you're going through or any pain you're experiencing. Those experiences and your feelings are real. Yet . . . when we turn our thoughts to Jesus and consider the amazing truth of Who He is and what He's done, we find comfort, hope, encouragement and strength to continue on in this fallen world.

When you're feeling down, I pray that you'll turn to Christ for comfort and strength. He is your Creator. He loves you enough to have given His earthly life on your behalf so that your sins could be forgiven and you could enjoy eternal life with Jesus. Praise God!

Reflection Questions:

CHAPTER 30: COMFORT IN CHRIST

1. How does knowing Who Jesus is - God, Creator, the Second Person of the Holy Trinity - help you to draw closer to Him?
2. When you consider all that Jesus has done for you, how does this affect you and your perspective about your trials?
3. Does it comfort you to know that Jesus went through suffering during His incarnation, and so He understands how you feel?
4. What are some examples of Jesus (prophecy, Christophany, foreshadowing, etc.) that you see in the Old Testament?

Afterword: Hold On to His Promises

As we wind up our 30 days together, I pray that your hope, perseverance, and strength have been renewed by God's Word that we've studied here. I realize that the challenges you're facing aren't easy, yet with Jesus by our side we're given patience and endurance to withstand these trials.

Whenever you feel overwhelmed by challenges, I hope that you'll stop and pray for God's help. I also pray that you'll read the Bible daily, as Scripture is living and active (Hebrews 4:12). God's Word is powerful and it never returns void. God's Word shall accomplish God's purpose and shall succeed in the purpose for which God sent it (c.f., Isaiah 55:11). God's Word is a lamp for our feet and a light on our path (c.f., Psalm 119:105).

God is so good to us, often in ways we can't see or don't notice. I find it uplifting to thank God for everyone and everything for which I'm grateful. Making a gratitude list keeps me focused upon my blessings, and reminds me to thank God for His kindness, protection, and provision.

May we trust that God allows us to face these challenges for His purpose and for our ultimate good. May our greatest aims be about drawing nearer to God. May we praise God always, including during life's storms!

All glory to God, Doreen

About the Author

Doreen Virtue holds a Master's degree in Biblical and Theological Studies with highest honors from Western Seminary, and a Master's and Bachelor's in Counseling Psychology from Chapman University. God saved Doreen out of new age and new thought deception in 2017. She is devoted to encouraging Christian women, especially those who've been saved out of deception, and pointing them to the Gospel and Bible study.

You can connect with me on:
- https://doreenvirtue.com
- https://x.com/DoreenVirtue
- https://www.facebook.com/DoreenVirtueForJesus
- https://www.instagram.com/doreenvirtue
- https://www.youtube.com/@Doreen_Virtue

Also by Doreen Virtue

Encouraging and comforting biblically solid books for Christian women, available in Kindle and paperback at Amazon.com/Shop/DoreenVirtue

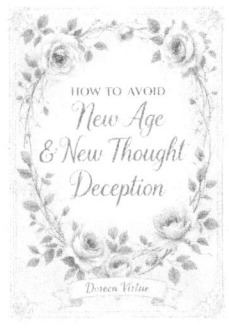

How to Avoid New Age & New Thought Deception

https://www.amazon.com/shop/doreenvirtue

This practical biblically sound guide helps Christian women to navigate away from New Age and New Thought deception, which is unfortunately so prevalent in the world right now. Doreen Virtue, who was born and raised in New Thought churches for 33 years, and who later segued into New Age deception for 26 years before God mercifully saved her at age 59, offers an insider view to help you to spot and avoid these false teachings.

In this book, you'll learn:

- Red flags to alert you when something is New Age or New Thought.
- The false promises that these deceptions use to lure people in.
- Why New Age and New Thought appeal to vulnerable women, and how to resist any temptation.
- Why Christian freedom and liberty doesn't give us license to engage in condemned practices.
- What the Bible says about New Age and New Thought teachings.
- Which items in your home to discard right away, to protect yourself and your family from New Age and New Thought influences.
- The top New Age and New Thought deceptions that are tragically creeping into local churches.
- The real reasons why yoga (including "Christian yoga") is spiritually harmful.
- How trauma survivors and those with trust or control issues are more susceptible to New Age and New Thought teachings.
- What types of New Age and New Thought practitioners to avoid, and why.

Written in a warm, compassionate, and comforting style, this book is also a helpful resource for your own evangelism to those who are currently in New Age or New Thought deception. This book would also make a great gift to warn your loved ones about these subtle-yet-destructive deceptions.

  Doreen Virtue holds a Master's Degree with highest honors in Biblical and Theological Studies from Western Seminary, and also a Master's and Bachelor's in Counseling Psychology from Chapman University. Doreen was graciously saved out of New Thought and New Age deception in 2017, and she encourages women with the Gospel and pointing them to Bible study.

Armor of God: Biblical Help for Spiritual Warfare 30-Day Devotional for Christian Women

This gentle 30-day devotional for women offers biblically solid teachings about how to deal with spiritual warfare, including guilt and shame about past sins; accusations from the enemy; insomnia, nightmares, or sleep paralysis; and how to distinguish between spiritual warfare and God's pruning process. You'll examine each of the elements of the Armor of God, and read encouraging Scripture to help you during seasons of struggle.

Comfort in Christ Devotional & Coloring Book

https://www.amazon.com/shop/doreenvirtue

Here's a relaxing way to dive deeper into your favorite comforting verses, as you color pages with Scripture. Each coloring page is accompanied by a biblically solid devotional in a large 14-point font.

Psalm 23 Devotional & Coloring Book

Adorable lambs and biblically solid devotional pages help you to memorize and dive deeper in the comforting verses of Psalm 23 in the classic King James Version. This devotional and coloring book is Gospel-centered, and suitable for adults and children.

Biblical Truth about Angels: What the Bible Really Says about Angels and Archangels

After being saved out of false new age and new thought teachings about angels, Doreen went to seminary and earned a Master's Degree with highest honors. While in seminary, Doreen researched every part of the Bible that describes angels. In "Biblical Truth about Angels," you'll read what the Bible really says about God's angels.

Forgiving Who Hurt You
Guided Prayer Journal & Devotional

The Bible commands us to forgive as we are forgiven. Yet, how do we forgive someone who has deeply hurt us?

In the **Forgiving Who Hurt You** guided prayer journal & devotional, you'll be walked through the process of leaning into God's strength, wisdom, and love to forgive what seems to be unforgivable.

This beautifully illustrated journal has lots of white lined spaces to write your thoughts about each devotional, and to journal about your prayers, fears, anxieties, and other issues to bring to God.

With God's strength, we can leave behind bitterness and anger. Forgiveness doesn't mean that we agree with what happened, or that we need to be friends with those who hurt us. We choose to forgive because of our love and obedience to God, and how He mercifully forgave us when we were saved.

Printed in Dunstable, United Kingdom